CHRISTMAS CRAFTS

CHRISTMAS CRAFTS

Carol McCleeve

*Easy-to-make cards, gift wrappings
and decorations for all the family*

Sterling Publishing Co., Inc. New York

CARDS &
GIFT
WRAPPINGS

Shopping for cards and gift wrappings can be a frustrating experience. Many cards look mass-produced and uninspiring, and gift boxes and wrapping paper can end up costing almost as much as the presents themselves. This chapter demonstrates how to make your own cards and gift wrappings using inexpensive and readily available materials that will delight your family and friends at the same time! They will also appreciate the fact that you have taken the time and trouble especially for them.

For highly individual wrappings, turn your hand to decorating your own wrapping papers. The range of possibilities is enormous, from sturdy brown wrapping paper to ephemeral-looking tissue papers in every colour in the rainbow, from pulpy newsprint to wonderfully textured varieties crafted by hand. Boxes made from a simple template and a brightly coloured conical container are just two of the gift-wrapping options demonstrated here. The boxes can be kept long after the festive season is over and used to store precious keepsakes and souvenirs. With a little time and imagination, you can produce creative gift wrappings that will leave your family and friends gasping with admiration.

All the designs in this chapter are based around a range of attractive seasonal stencils. Experiment with different colours and materials to find out what works best. Once you've discovered how easy it is to make your own cards and gift wrappings, you'll never want to go back to the store-bought variety again!

LEFT: *An array of brightly coloured cards, gift boxes and wrapping papers, made using the simple stencil motifs on pages 26–34. It is surprising how different a design can look when you simply change the colour combination or use a different type of paper.*

Making A Card & Envelope

*It is always much nicer to receive a hand-made Christmas card
than a mass-produced one and you will find that people really
appreciate the effort and care that you have put into making them.
A template for a square card appears on page 24, but here you can see
how to make a card to any shape or size you choose.*

MAKING THE CARDS

1 Using a ruler or straightedge, draw a horizontal line twice the width of the card. Using a set square, draw vertical lines for the left and right edges and the centre fold.

2 Draw a horizontal line for the top edge of the card. (Use a set square to check that the corners are accurate.)

3 Using a metal-edged ruler and scalpel, carefully cut around the outline of the card.

4 Place the card on a cutting mat, right side down. Turn the scalpel over so that the blade is uppermost and lightly score along the centre fold. Don't press too hard or you will cut right through.

5 Rub out the pencil marks and crease along the centre fold line. The card is now ready for decorating.

RIGHT: *All these cards were made using the stencil designs on pages 26–30. To make your cards look even more individual, try adding a few ribbon curls or a delicate lace edging, or sprinkling on a little glitter for a festive finish.*

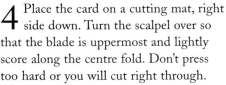

MAKING THE ENVELOPE

BELOW: *The envelope should be ⅛ in (3 mm) bigger all round than the card. A template for an envelope to fit a square card is given on page 25, but you may need to adjust it.*

1 Adjust the template on page 25 to fit your card if necessary, then trace the template onto tracing paper and rub a soft pencil over the traced lines.

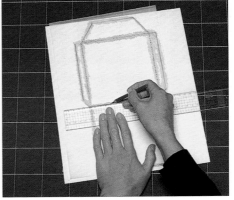

2 Turn the tracing paper over and place it on the paper you are going to use for the envelope. Using a ruler and an HB pencil, draw over the lines to transfer them to the envelope paper.

3 Using a metal-edged ruler and a scalpel, carefully cut around the outline of the envelope.

4 Turn the scalpel over and use the blunt side to score along the dotted lines. The dotted lines indicate where you will fold in the side and top flaps in step 6. Rub out any pencil marks.

5 Turn the envelope over and place double-sided tape along the side flaps. Trim off the excess tape. Peel off the backing paper using the tip of the scalpel blade.

6 Turn the envelope over again, press in the side flaps so the tape is uppermost.

7 Fold up the envelope to form a pocket. Press down onto the double-sided tape.

CUTTING THE STENCIL

BELOW: *Stencils can be cut from a variety of materials. From top to bottom: manila card, K-trace (drawing film) and acetate. Manila card is inexpensive and easy to cut. It is opaque and it can be difficult to line up separate overlays if you are using several colours. K-trace (drawing film) can be re-used many times, as you can wipe off the paint. Acetate is similar to K-trace, but it is more expensive and not as easy to cut.*

1 Using a hard pencil, trace your chosen design onto tracing paper. A selection of stencil designs for both cards and wrapping papers is given on pages 26–30.

2 Rub a soft pencil over the traced lines, making sure that you cover every single one.

3 Turn the tracing paper over and place it on your stencil material. Trace over the design again with a hard pencil to transfer the design to the stencil material.

4 Place the stencil material on a cutting mat or a piece of thick cardboard and carefully cut around the design with a sharp scalpel.

RIGHT: *You can apply stencils to almost any type of paper, from thick glossy card to hand-made rag papers and delicate, semi-transparent tissue paper. A good paper supplier will stock an incredible variety of colours and types. Experiment to see what effects you can achieve.*

APPLYING COLOUR

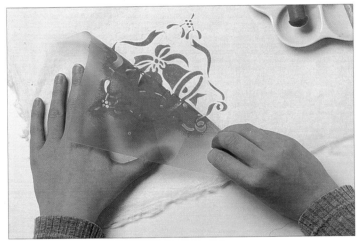

1 Position the cut-out stencil on your chosen paper and press down firmly so that the stencil cannot slip. Hold the stencil brush almost upright and dab paint through the stencil.

2 Carefully peel back the stencil so that the paint does not smudge. Leave to dry. Water-based paint dries in minutes, but oil-based painting sticks can take up to 48 hours.

LEFT: *Essential stencilling equipment. Bristle stencil brushes are best: they come in a range of sizes. Stencil paints can be water based or oil based stencil painting sticks. To use painting sticks, rub them onto a china palette or dish, as here, and then pick up the paint on your brush as normal.*

3 When the paint is dry, attach a tiny square of double-sided tape to each corner of the stencilled paper. Remove the backing paper and position on a ready-made card.

Victorian-Style Card

This pretty little Victorian-style card, with a lift-up flat that conceals a message for the special person in your life, makes a wonderful Christmas keepsake.

MATERIALS

Stencils (see page 26)

•

Card/thin cardboard

•

Green and red stencil paint

•

Pencil

•

Double-sided tape

•

Scalpel

1 Using the stencil for the rectangular border at the foot of page 26, apply red paint to everything except the holly leaves in the corners.

ABOVE: *In this design, two colours are used. You must take care not to move the stencil when applying the second colour.*

2 When the red paint is dry, apply green paint to the holly leaves. Leave to dry.

3 Put the stencilled paper on a cutting mat and, using a scalpel, carefully cut around the decorative shaped edges of the stencilled design.

4 Cut a piece of card (cardboard) the same size as the blank rectangle within the stencilled design and stencil the holly motif from page 26 onto it.

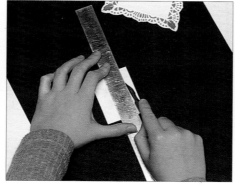

5 Draw a pencil line slightly below one long edge of the small piece of card (cardboard). Score along it using the reverse side of the scalpel blade.

6 Place double-sided tape along the scored edge and peel off the backing paper. Stick the small piece of card (cardboard) in the centre of the rectangle.

Collage Card

The addition of red and green ribbon curls and tiny gold bows creates a very effective three-dimensional effect. The stencil for this Christmas wreath is on page 27.

MATERIALS

White tissue paper
•
Stencil (see page 27)
•
Red, pink, gold and green stencil sticks or paints
•
Stencilling brush
•
Pre-made glossy white card
•
All-purpose glue
•
4 gold ribbon bows
•
Red and green ribbon curls (see page 127)

ABOVE: *This four-colour wreath design is stencilled onto white tissue paper which is then stuck onto a glossy white card. Use a detail from the same stencil to make an attractive matching envelope.*

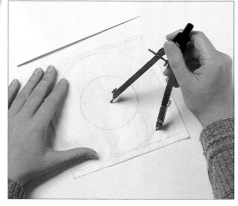

1 Using a pair of compasses, draw circles 3 and 6 in (7.5 and 15 cm) in diameter on a piece of white tissue paper to mark the inner and outer edges of the wreath.

2 Using the first overlay, stencil the rose hips and some of the roses in red. Peel back. Place the second overlay in position and apply pink paint to some of the remaining roses. Peel back.

3 Using the third overlay, apply gold paint to the remaining roses.

4 Using the fourth overlay, stencil the holly and ivy leaves in green. Then, keeping as close as you can to the outer edge of the design, carefully cut out the stencilled motif.

5 Stick the stencilled tissue paper onto a pre-made glossy white card, making sure you keep the tissue paper smooth. Glue tiny ribbon curls and gold bows around the wreath.

Lace-Edged Card

Lining and edging are sophisticated finishing touches which make your cards look as if they have been given that all-important extra care and attention.

RIGHT: *This card was made by combining several of the stencil motifs shown on page 27, with a lace trim around the edge as a additional refinement. The lining paper should be about $1/8$ in (3 mm) smaller on all sides than the card so that it does not protrude beyond the card's edges.*

1 Stick double-sided tape along the edges of the reverse side of the stencilled paper. Peel off the backing paper, attach thin lace, then glue the stencilled paper to a pre-made card.

2 Place a small amount of all-purpose glue along the central fold of the inside of the card.

3 Cut the lining paper to the right size, then fold it in half and press its central fold onto the glue. Do not close the card until the glue has dried, otherwise you may glue it shut.

MATERIALS

Double-sided tape
•
Stencilled paper
•
Thin lace
•
Pre-made card
•
All-purpose glue
•
Tissue or other very thin paper for lining

Decorating Wrapping Papers

Stencilling is one of the easiest ways of decorating a large expanse of paper. These two projects show how to stencil om soft tissue paper and how to texture the paper before you apply the paint.

MATERIALS

Tissue paper
•
Stencil (see pages 31–34)
•
Stencil sticks or paints
•
Stencilling brush

STENCILLING TISSUE PAPER

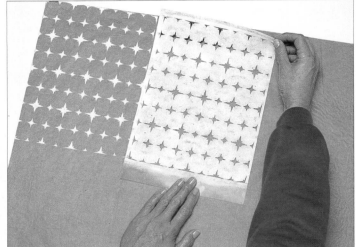

1 Place your stencil on the tissue paper and stipple paint through the holes. Carefully lift up the stencil, making sure you don't crease the tissue paper, and reposition it, lining it up with the pattern you have already laid down.

2 Repeat until you have covered the whole paper, then leave to dry. This will take anything from a couple of hours to 1-2 days, depending on the type of paint you have used, and the paper should remain completely flat during this time.

TEXTURING PAPER

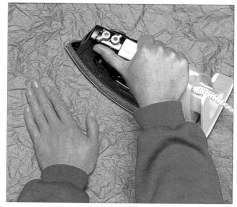

1 Take a sheet of strong brown wrapping paper and scrunch it into a ball, pressing it firmly to crease it and break the sizing (protective coating) that covers the shiny side.

2 Flatten the paper out with your hands and iron it, shiny side down, with the iron on a low setting, working outwards from the middle to prevent it from curling.

3 Place your chosen stencil in the top left corner of the paper and apply the paint. Continue until you have covered the whole paper, then leave to dry.

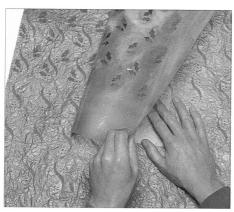

4 Take the second stencil overlay and position it carefully on the paper. Then stipple through the stencil using your second paint colour.

5 Continue in this way until you have completely covered the paper, then leave to dry.

MATERIALS

Strong brown wrapping paper

•

Iron

•

Stencil (see pages 31–34)

•

Stencil sticks or paints

•

Stencilling brush

BELOW: *You can stencil onto any type of paper – tissue, crepe, or even plain brown wrapping paper. Choose a paper to complement the type of present you are giving: tissue paper, for example, is ideal for wrapping a delicate silk scarf or a fragile gift such as china, while sturdy wrapping paper would be more appropriate for a heavy box. The stencils for all the designs shown here can be found on pages 31–34.*

Christmas Gift Box

On the next six pages, you will find a selection of ideas for making and decorating gift boxes and containers. The template for this box is given on page 35. To alter the size, simply increase or reduce the template on a photocopier.

MATERIALS

HB pencil
•
Tracing paper
•
4B pencil
•
10 x 5 in (25 x 12.5 cm) piece of cardboard
•
Metal ruler
•
Scalpel
•
Cutting mat
•
Double-sided tape

ABOVE: *A red-and-green ribbon provides an elegant finishing touch to this simply made gift box. You could also make a matching gift tag, using a leftover piece of cardboard.*

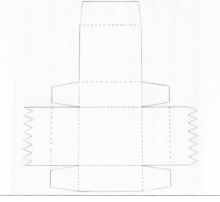

1 Using an HB pencil, trace the template on page 35 onto tracing paper. The dotted lines on the template indicate where the folds will be.

2 Rub a soft 4B pencil over the traced lines, making sure that you cover both the internal and the external lines.

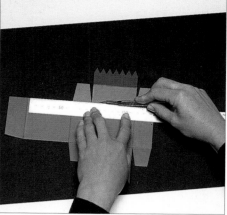

3 Turn the tracing paper over and place it on top of the cardboard you have chosen for your box. Using a ruler and the HB pencil, draw over the traced lines.

4 Put the cardboard on a cutting mat and, using a scalpel and a metal ruler, carefully cut around the outside edges of the traced lines.

5 Using the reverse side of the scalpel blade, lightly score along the dotted lines. Take care not to press too hard on the scalpel or you will cut right through the cardboard.

RIGHT: *Plain dark green cardboard was used to make this box. The serrated edges on the inner flaps are an unusual touch, allowing you to catch an intriguing glimpse of the gift inside.*

6 Press along the fold lines. Place a piece of double-sided tape on each of the four flaps (marked with a cross on the template on page 35). Peel off the backing tape.

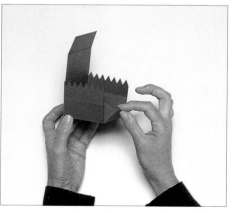

7 Fold up the flaps and press them tightly against the sides of the box to fix them firmly in position. The box is now ready to be filled and decorated.

19

Lined Box

To protect breakable gifts and to give your boxes an added touch of sophistication, line them with a piece of soft tissue paper in a pretty contrasting colour.

MATERIALS

16-in (40-cm) square of stencilled cardboard

•

Double-sided tape

•

12-in (30-cm) square of tissue paper

•

Wired chiffon ribbon to decorate

•

Twig and berry bunch to decorate (see pages 62–63)

ABOVE: *This box is adapted from the template on page 35. To reinforce the box and make it firmer, the flaps are the same size as the sides of the box. Brighten it up by adding extra decorations. Here a white chiffon ribbon bow and a twig and berry bunch (see pages 62–63) completes the decoration.*

1 Cut out the box shape and score along the fold lines. With the patterned side of the cardboard uppermost, place double-sided tape along the top left and right side flaps.

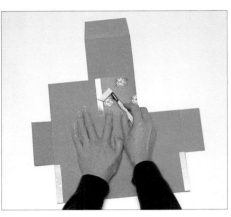

2 Turn the cardboard over and place double-sided tape on the reverse side of the bottom left and right flaps. Using the tip of a scalpel, peel off the backing paper from the double-sided tape.

3 Lift up the back of the box, align the flaps on the fold lines and bring up the front of the box to meet them. Press the flaps against the box to secure.

4 Place strips of double-sided tape on the sides of the box, peel off the backing paper, fold up the sides and press firmly to fix in place.

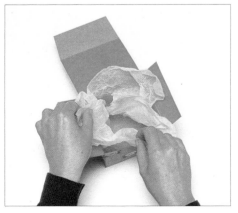

5 Place a piece of double-sided tape inside the box and peel off the backing paper. Gently scrunch up the tissue paper and press it onto the tape to hold it in place.

Christmas Cone

This open cone, with its ribbon loop for hanging, makes an attractive container for candies or other small gifts. Make miniature versions to hang on the Christmas tree.

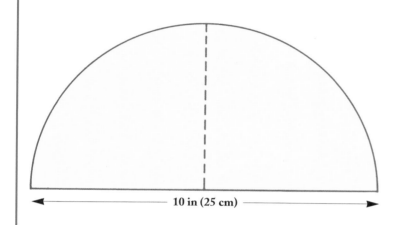

◄—— 10 in (25 cm) ——►

MATERIALS

12-in (30-cm) square of stiff stencilled paper

•

Magic tape

•

5 x 4 in (12.5 x 10 cm) strip of crepe paper for streamers

•

Paper glue

•

2 pieces of 20 x 1 in (50 x 2.5 cm) crepe paper for frill

•

Cotton thread

•

Double-sided tape

•

12-in (30-cm) length of ribbon, ¹/₈ in (3 mm) wide

LEFT: *Children, in particular, will love these colourful cones. Make lots of them for a children's Christmas party so that each guest has one to take home.*

1 Draw a circle 5 in (12.5 cm) in radius on stencilled paper. Cut it out, then fold it in half and cut along the fold line to make a semi-circle.

2 Fold the semi-circle in half with the stencilled design on the inside and press firmly to leave a crisp fold line.

3 Unfold the semi-circle. With the straight edge furthest away from you, curve the paper inwards from one edge until the straight edge aligns with the centre fold, top and bottom.

LEFT: *These miniature versions of the cones are about 3¹/₂ in (8 cm) tall and would make lovely tree decorations. Make sure, however, that whatever you put inside them is very light – otherwise the cones may weigh down the branches. Here, the open ends of the cones are trimmed with scraps of lace, which gives them a more delicate, feminine appeal.*

4 Roll the paper around the base of the cone from the other corner until the remainder of the straight edge aligns with the centre fold, top and bottom. Hold firmly in place.

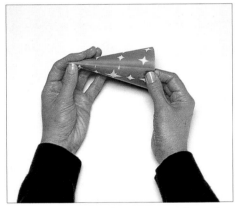

5 Place a piece of magic tape along the length of the centre fold to secure seam of the cone.

6 Gently rub a scalpel handle or your thumb nail over the magic tape to burnish it. This makes the tape less noticeable and ensures that it is properly attached to the cone.

7 To make the streamers, take a 5 x 4 in (12.5 x 10 cm) piece of crepe paper and fold it in half three times to give eight layers.

8 Make three evenly spaced cuts along the length of the paper, stopping about 1/2 in (1 cm) from the top.

9 To make an opening for inserting the cxrepe paper streamers, cut off the tip of the cone about 1/8 in (3 mm) from the tip. Twist the uncut end of crepe paper to form a fine point and insert it into the tip of the cone.

10 Put a dab of glue on the inside of the cone. Use a pencil or scalpel tip to hold the streamers in place for a few moments to secure.

11 To make the frill, take two pieces of crepe paper measuring 20 x 1 in (50 x 2.5 cm). Place one on top of the other and tack together with double cotton along the length of the crepe paper strip.

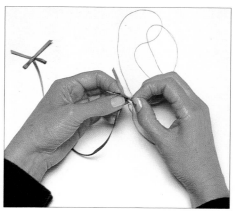

12 Pull the cotton to gather the frill evenly to a length of about 8 in (20 cm). Attach around the outer edge of the cone with small pieces of double-sided tape.

13 Cut an 8-in (20-cm) length of ribbon. Make two small bows from the remaining ribbon and stitch one to each end of the long ribbon.

14 Glue the ribbon to the centre back and centre front of the cone to form a loop for carrying or hanging. The cone is now ready to fill with candies or small trinkets.

Card & Envelope Templates

Dotted line indicates fold

LEFT: *This template makes a card which measures 4¹/₂ x 4¹/₂ in (112 x 112 mm). To alter the size, simply increase or reduce the size of the template on a photocopier. Instructions on how to make a card can be found on page 8. The basic card can then be decorated with any of the stencil motifs on pages 26–30.*

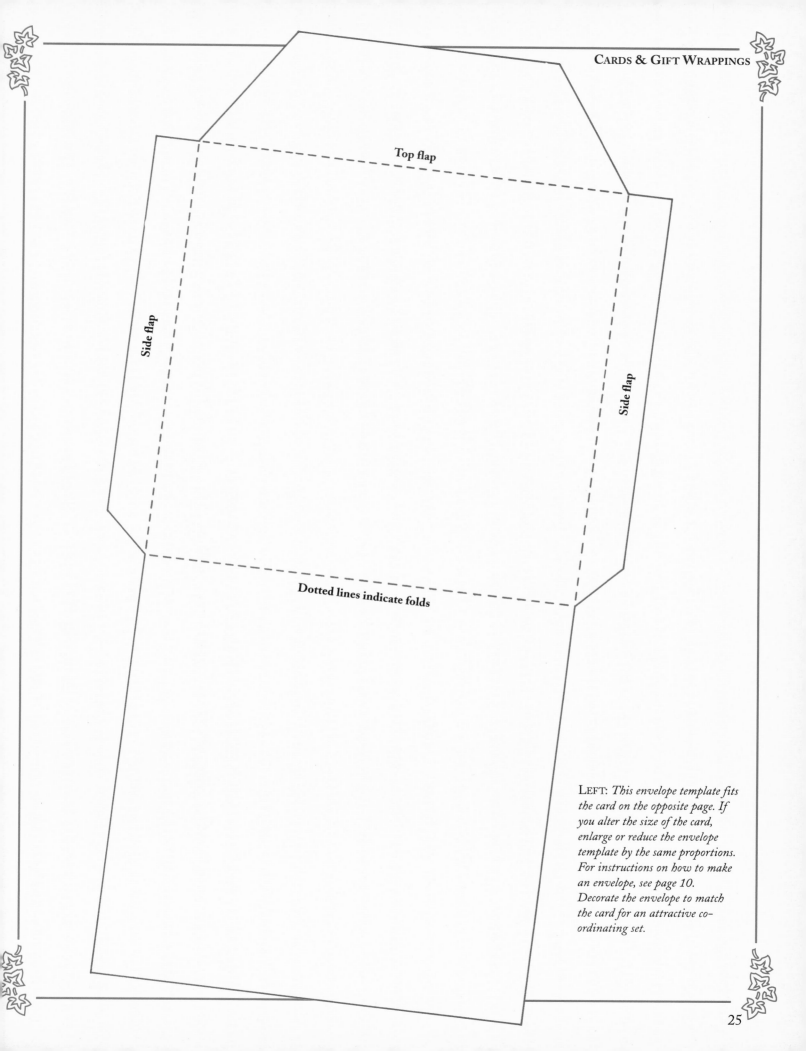

Top flap

Side flap

Side flap

Dotted lines indicate folds

LEFT: *This envelope template fits the card on the opposite page. If you alter the size of the card, enlarge or reduce the envelope template by the same proportions. For instructions on how to make an envelope, see page 10. Decorate the envelope to match the card for an attractive co-ordinating set.*

Stencil Motifs

"DING DONG MERRILY ON HIGH!"

LEFT: *This attractive bell design can be worked in one or several colours. For a pretty finishing touch, stipple white paint over the stencil design when dry to give the impression of falling snow.*

VICTORIAN NOSTALGIA

BELOW: *This motif was used to make the border for the Victorian-style card, with the lift-up flap, shown on page 13.*

BELOW: *This motif forms the design for the lift-up flap on the Victorian-style card on page 13.*

CHRISTMAS WREATH

RIGHT: *The Christmas wreath is a complicated stencil using four overlays of colour (see page 14). Cut a separate stencil for each colour following the key below.*

Red ————
Pink ··········
Gold —·—·—·
Green ————

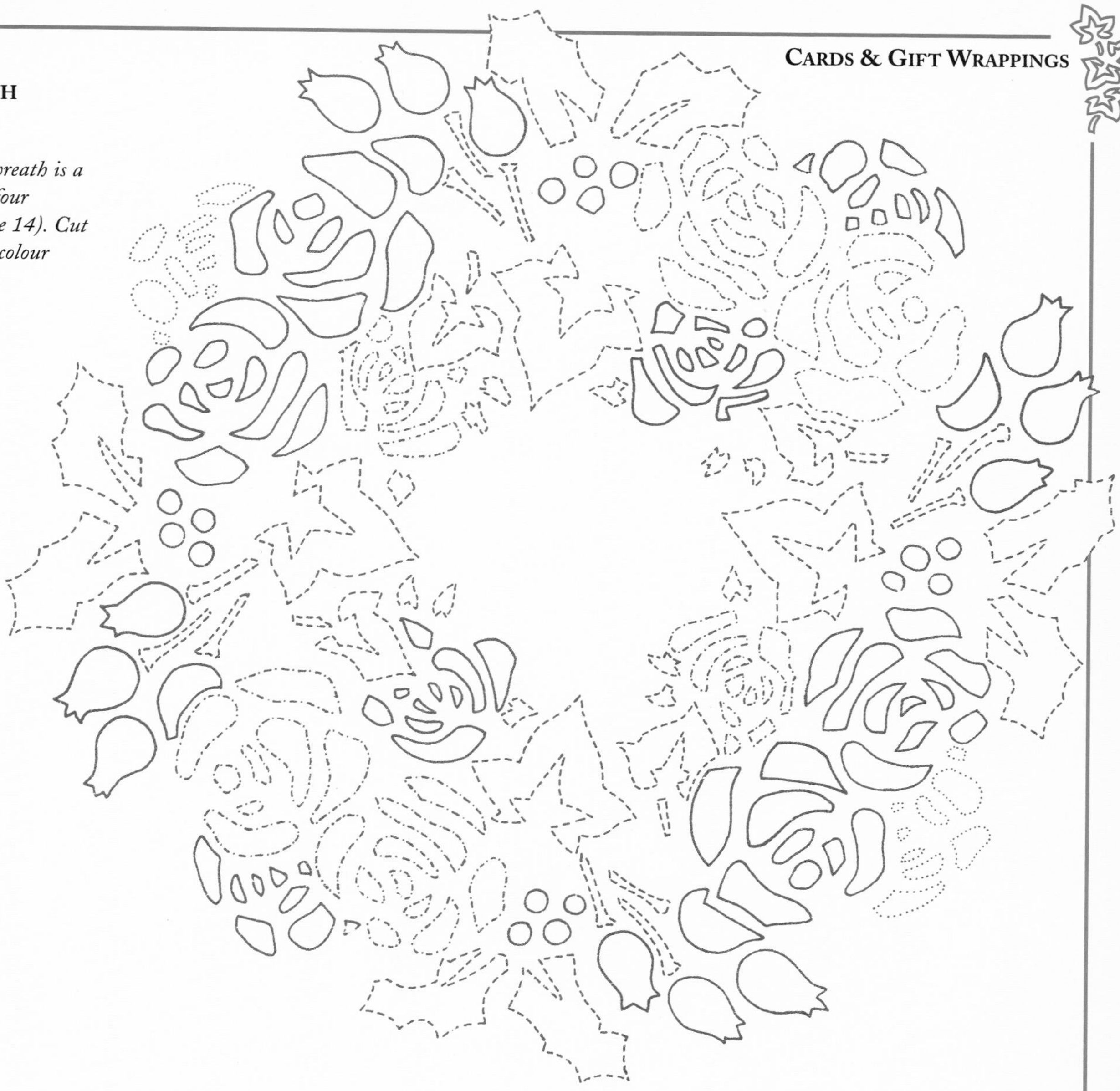

FLORAL FEAST

Holly, ivy, rose hips and roses – a feast of flowers and foliage to brighten up any Christmas card. Use individual stencils as details for envelopes or gift tags, or combine several in a design of your own making.

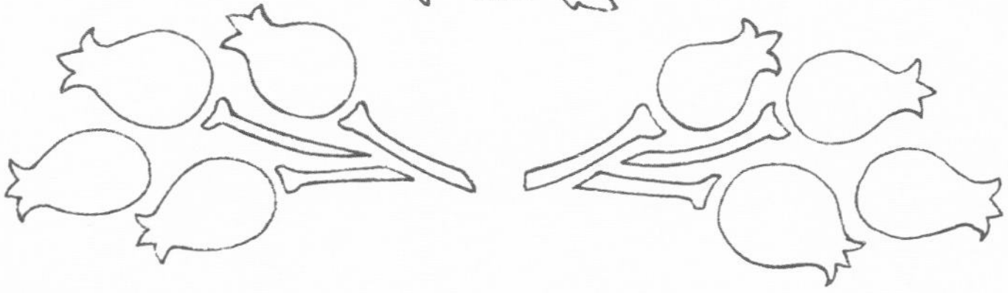

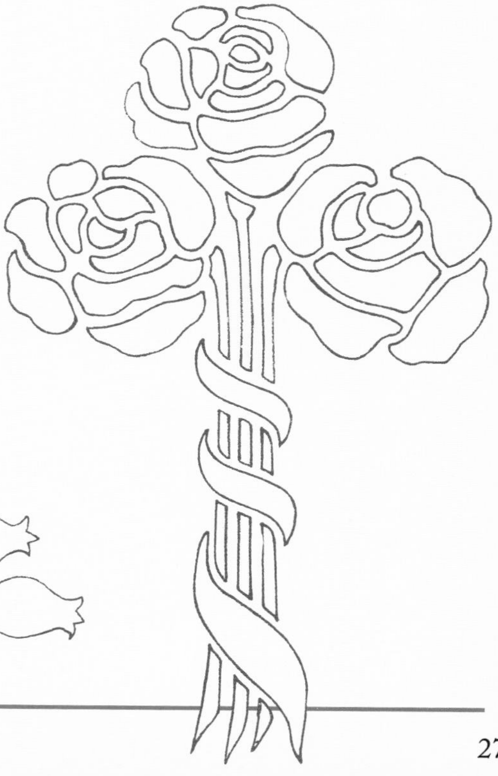

FESTIVE FUN

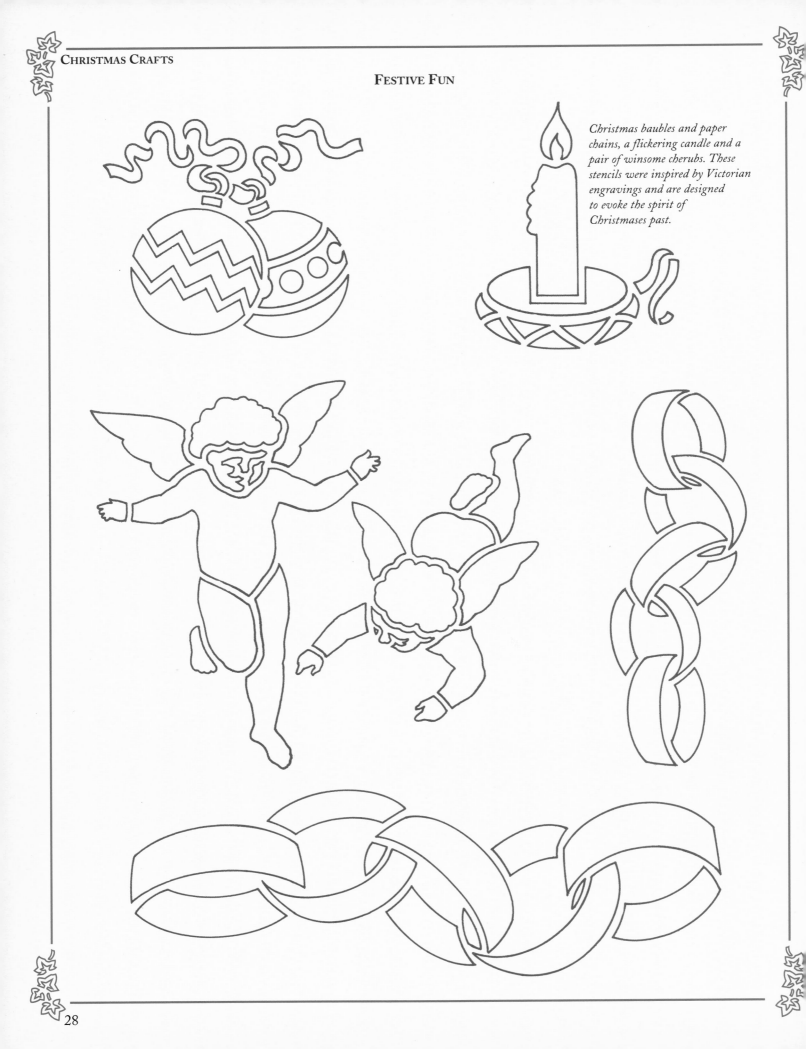

Christmas baubles and paper chains, a flickering candle and a pair of winsome cherubs. These stencils were inspired by Victorian engravings and are designed to evoke the spirit of Christmases past.

SEASONAL SYMMETRY

The ordered symmetry of snowflakes and Christmas trees is always pleasing to the eye. Symmetrical designs look good as patterns repeated over a large area such as a sheet of wrapping paper.

CHRISTMAS MISCELLANY

A star in the night sky, a peal of bells, a chirpy robin and a pair of seasonal snowmen — all the trappings of a traditional Christmas.

POINSETTIA WRAPPING PAPER

HOLLY AND RIBBON WRAPPING PAPER

CHRISTMAS ROSE WRAPPING PAPER

STARBURST WRAPPING PAPER

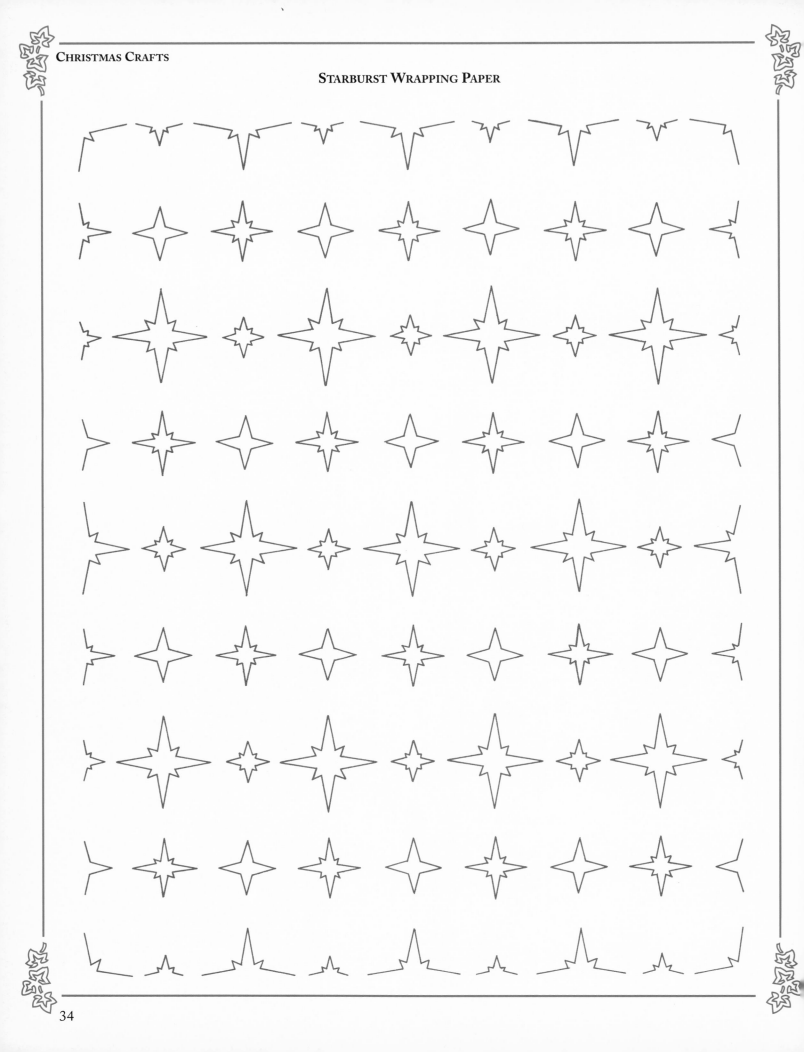

Box Template

Dotted lines indicate folds

LEFT: *This template makes a box measuring $2^3/4$ x $2^3/4$ x $1^1/4$ in (7 x 7 x 3 cm). To make a deeper box, increase the sides of the box (indicated by arrows on the template) by equal amounts. The four crosses indicate the side flaps. Place double-sided tape at these points to stick the box together.*

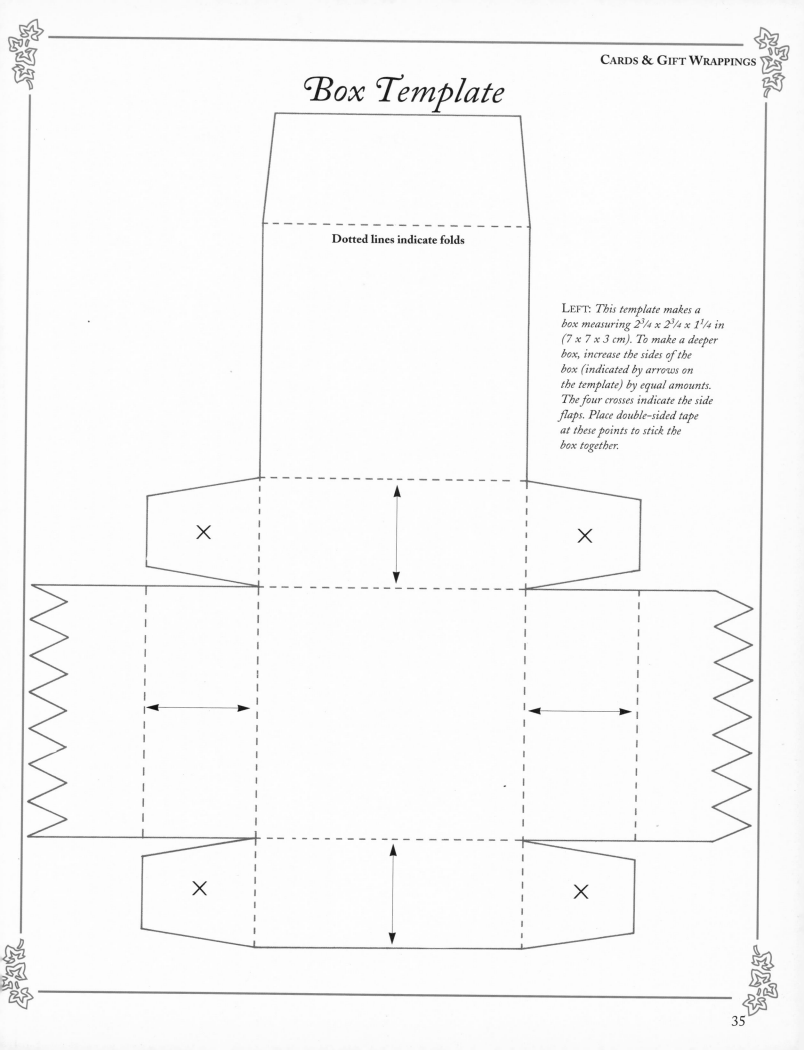

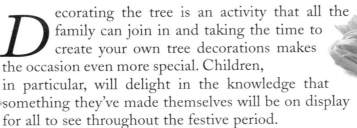

DECORATING THE TREE

Decorating the tree is an activity that all the family can join in and taking the time to create your own tree decorations makes the occasion even more special. Children, in particular, will delight in the knowledge that something they've made themselves will be on display for all to see throughout the festive period.

In this chapter you will find something to suit all ages and tastes, from a traditional-style fairy to grace the top of the tree to a brightly coloured lucky dip tub at the base. All the projects are very easy to make and the majority could be made by even quite young children under supervision. None requires any skill other than basic sewing and most of the materials are cheap and readily available around the home.

One idea in keeping with the Christmas spirit is for some of your tree decorations to double up as small gifts for your family and friends when they visit over the festive season, perhaps personalizing the design to suit the recipient, as in the scented cross-stitch sachets shown on pages 50–51. Edible gifts are always appreciated and the almond bunches demonstrated on page 42 are a particularly simple yet sophisticated-looking idea.

The decorative finishes shown in these projects are only suggestions: if you can't get hold of exactly the same trimmings, or if you would prefer different colours, feel free to experiment. You will have far more fun inventing your own designs.

LEFT: Bold felt shapes, miniature wreaths and almond bunches are just a few of the decorations demonstrated in this chapter. Ribbon curls add an essential touch of glamour amd sparkle.

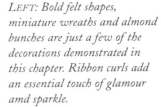

Tree Fairy

*This glittering tree fairy, with her sequin-studded wings and
gleaming white sash, would grace any traditional-style Christmas tree.
The project can be hand sewn or machine stitched.*

MATERIALS

For one fairy 7 in (17.5 cm) tall:

12-in (30-cm) square of pink felt for body

Matching thread

Kapok

Doll's hair

Black, blue and pink threads

Red sequin

Small white ribbon bow for hair

20 x 4 in (50 x 10 cm) piece of white net for wings

10 x 4 in (25 x 10 cm) piece of gold net for wings

30–40 gold star-shaped sequins

20 x 4 in (50 x 10 cm) strip of white net for the skirt

20 x 4 in (50 x 10 cm) strip of gold net for the skirt

20-in (50-cm) length of wired white chiffon ribbon for sash,
1½ in (4 cm) wide

LEFT: *Once you have made the tree fairy,
add a few finishing touches of your own
choosing. Here, a bead necklace, a chiffon
shoulder wrap, and a bow and sequin on
one ankle complete the decoration.*

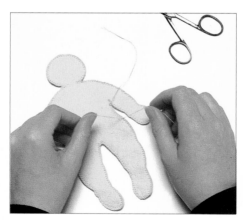

1 Cut out two body pieces and stitch
together, leaving a 1½-in (4-cm) gap
under one arm for the filling. Tie off any
loose threads.

2 Stuff with kapok, making sure the
filling is firm and evenly distributed.
Close the gap with tiny running stitches
and tie off any loose threads.

3 Arrange the doll's hair around the
head and secure with tiny running
stitches, taking care to stitch through only
one layer of fabric. Trim the hair to tidy
if necessary.

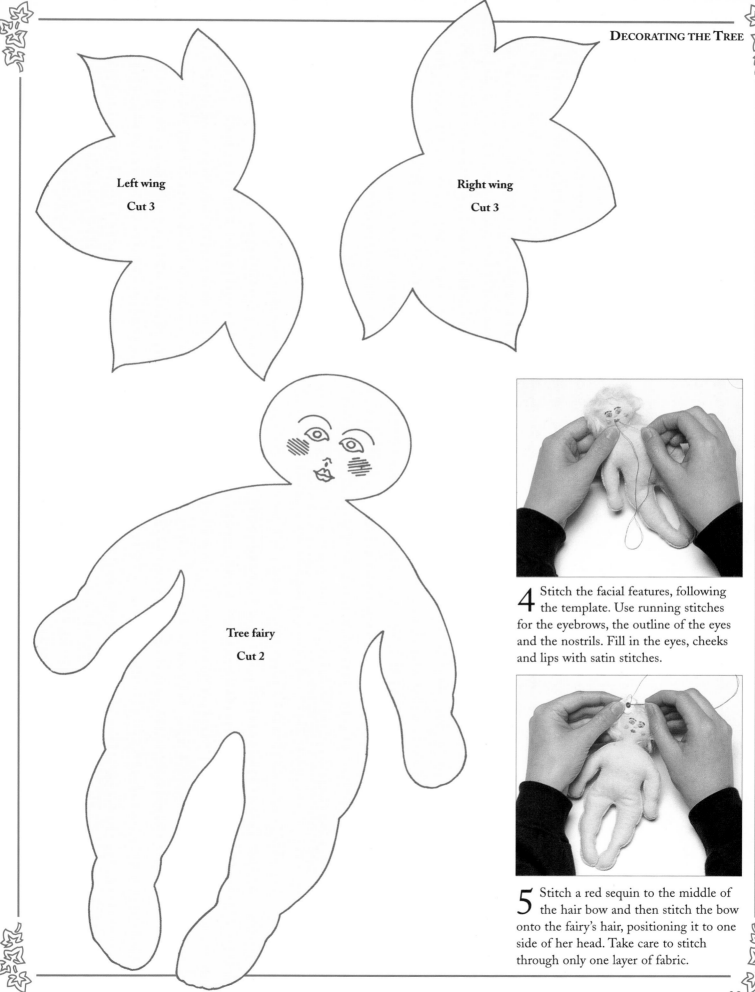

Left wing

Cut 3

Right wing

Cut 3

Tree fairy

Cut 2

4 Stitch the facial features, following the template. Use running stitches for the eyebrows, the outline of the eyes and the nostrils. Fill in the eyes, cheeks and lips with satin stitches.

5 Stitch a red sequin to the middle of the hair bow and then stitch the bow onto the fairy's hair, positioning it to one side of her head. Take care to stitch through only one layer of fabric.

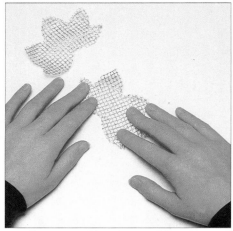  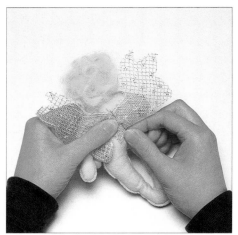

6 Cut one gold and two white pieces of net for each wing. Place the three pieces for each wing together, with the gold piece on top, and stitch all round keeping close to the edge.

7 Sew 15–20 gold star-shaped sequins onto the gold side of each wing, spacing them evenly. The sequins will sparkle as they catch the light.

8 Overlap the bases of the wings. Place them on the fairy's back, white sides uppermost, and secure with tiny stitches at the point of overlap and at the shoulders.

  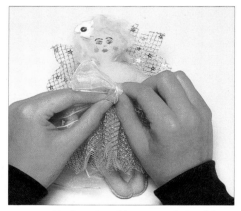

9 Place the two skirt pieces together, with the gold net on top, and tack along the top edge. Fold over three times and cut evenly spaced V-shapes along the bottom edge.

10 Run white gathering stitches along the top edge. Remove tacking stitches. Pull threads to gather the skirt to a length of approximately 3¹⁄₂ in (9 cm).

11 Gather the skirt around the fairy and fasten in place with a couple of running stitches. Tie wired chiffon ribbon around the fairy's waist in a neat bow to form the sash.

RIGHT: *Experiment with different colour combinations for the skirt and wings. Gold-spotted net on top of russet organza (right) is a rich, warm combination. For a cooler colour scheme, opt for a light and a dark shade of green net (far right).*

THE WAND

MATERIALS

5-in (12.5-cm) fine wooden skewer,
sprayed gold

•

All-purpose glue

•

Gold star

•

6-in (15-cm) length of white ribbon,
¼ in (6 mm) wide

•

12-in (30-cm) length of wired white
chiffon ribbon, 1½ in (4 cm) wide

RIGHT: *No self-respecting tree
fairy would be complete without a
wand. The colours used here – gold for
the star and white for the
ribbon – are chosen to echo the
colours of her skirt
and wings.*

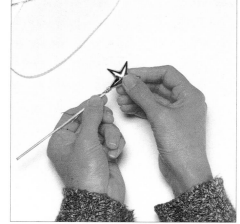

1 Cut off the sharp ends of the skewer. Put a generous dab of glue on one end and attach the star.

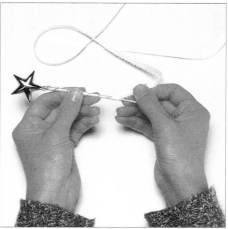

2 Glue the narrow white ribbon to one end of the skewer and twist it around the skewer in a spiral. Put a tiny dab of glue on the end of the ribbon to attach it to the skewer.

3 Tie a bow of wired white chiffon ribbon around the wand just underneath the star. Cut off any excess ribbon to neaten.

Almond Bunches

A few sugared almonds wrapped in coloured net make a sophisticated-looking tree decoration – with the added bonus that you can give them away to friends and visitors over the festive season.

MATERIALS

For each bunch:

Two 4-in (10-cm) squares of net in contrasting colours

•

3 sugared almonds

•

18-in (45-cm) length of ribbon, ¼ in (6 mm) wide

ABOVE: *Green and red net with an elegant gold ribbon. Green and red are complementary colours and always work well together. However, it is best to buy sugared almonds in delicate pastel shades such as white and pink so that they do not clash with the net wrapping.*

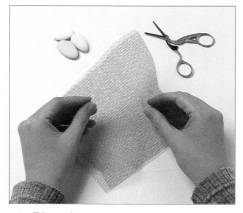

1 Place the two net squares one on top of the other.

2 Place the three almonds in the centre of the net squares and bring up the corners to form a neat bag.

3 Fold the ribbon in half and make a single stitch about 4 in (10 cm) from the fold. Hold the ribbon loop behind the almond bunch and tie the loose ends at the front in a bow.

LEFT: *Net is inexpensive and can be bought in small amounts. Buy a range of colours and experiment with different combinations so that each decoration is unique.*

Miniature Wreath

This miniature wreath is made from artificial leaves and berries, so if you store it carefully you will be able to use it year after year. Substitute dried or fresh leaves and berries if you prefer.

MATERIALS

For each bunch:

18-in (45-cm) length of red ribbon,
1/4 in (6 mm) wide
•
4-in (10-cm) wreath base,
available from florist's shops
•
All-purpose glue
•
3 small red ribbon bows
•
4 small bunches of artifical berries
•
Artificial green leaves
•
Small leaves such as hydrangea,
sprayed silver and gold

1 Make a loop at one end of the ribbon and secure with a single stitch. Wind ribbon around the wreath base and glue in place, snipping off excess. Glue on the three red ribbon bows.

2 Glue the bunches of artificial berries and green leaves at equal distances around the wreath.

3 Glue on gold and silver hydrangea leaves wherever necessary, making sure that the wreath base cannot be seen.

RIGHT: *For a touch of extra colour and sparkle, liven up the wreath by gluing on a few ribbon curls. The exact position of the decorations is not crucial, but you should try to make sure that the wreath base is fully covered.*

Christmas Trees

*These felt Christmas trees are only 3½ in (9 cm) tall and require
very little fabric. You can make them from pieces of felt left over
from the large stockings on pages 96–100.*

MATERIALS

For each tree:

4 x 8 in (10 x 20 cm) piece of green felt

•

14-in (35-cm) length of green ribbon, ¼ in (6 mm)
wide, for loop

•

5-in (12.5-cm) length of red ribbon, ¼ in (6 mm) wide

•

5-in (12.5-cm) length of silver ribbon, ¼ in (6 mm) wide

•

3 decorative sequins or beads

•

10 silver star-shaped sequins

•

1 red ribbon bow

LEFT: *If you are using plain felt, as
here, you will probably want to liven
it up a little by adding some
sparkly decorations. Star-shaped
sequins are perfect: they look
Christmassy and will catch the light
as the decoration twists and
turns on the tree.*

1 Cut two tree pieces from green felt,
using the template opposite, and
stitch together around the edges. Fasten
off any loose threads.

2 Fold the loop ribbon in half and
stitch to the top of the tree about
2½ in (6 cm) from the fold. Tie the loose
ends in a neat bow.

3 Stitch red ribbon to the outermost
points of the top branches of the
tree, twisting the ribbon once or twice in
the middle. Repeat with silver ribbon
across the second row of branches.

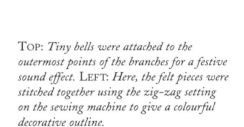

Cut 2

TOP: *Tiny bells were attached to the outermost points of the branches for a festive sound effect.* LEFT: *Here, the felt pieces were stitched together using the zig-zag setting on the sewing machine to give a colourful decorative outline.*

4 Stitch decorative sequins to the outermost points of the top branches and to the middle of the red ribbon twist.

5 Stitch star-shaped silver sequins to the outermost points of the middle branches and to the middle of the silver ribbon twist. Stitch more sequins onto the tree, spacing them evenly.

6 Complete the decoration by stitching a small red ribbon bow to the middle of the tree trunk, trimming off the ends on the diagonal.

Tree Stockings

These decorations are miniature versions of the stockings on pages 96–100. Fill them with small presents such as tiny toys for the children or foil-wrapped chocolates before you hang them on the tree.

MATERIALS

For each stocking:

12-in (30-cm) square of gold-spotted red felt for main stocking pieces

•

6 x 2 in (15 x 5 cm) piece of gold-spotted white felt for cuff

•

5-in (12.5-cm) length of gold ribbon, ¼-in (6-mm) wide, for cuff edging

•

5 white pearl beads

•

14-in (35-cm) length of gold ribbon, ¼-in (6-mm) wide, for loop

ABOVE: *The plain red felt used for the main stocking piece cried out for a flamboyant style of decoration, and so ribbon bows in three colours – green, red and silver – were used.*

ABOVE: *A red bow and a green loop with tiny bells attached provide the finishing touches to this stocking. Festive-looking baubles will give your Christmas decorations their individuality and style.*

LEFT: *Felt is available in a huge range of seasonal colours and patterns. The gold-spotted felt used here is perfect for Christmas decorations. It has such a lovely sparkle to it that very little is needed in the way of finishing touches.*

1 Cut two stocking pieces from the template below. Stitch together by hand or machine, stitching close to the edge, leaving the top open. Tie off any loose threads.

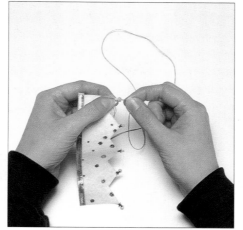

2 Cut one cuff piece from the template below. Fold in four, lengthways. Cut a V-shape into the bottom edge. Open out and stitch gold ribbon along long straight edge. Stitch a pearl bead to each V.

3 Stitch the cuff to the top of the stocking, aligning the short ends of the cuff with the back seam. Tie off any loose threads.

4 Fold the loop ribbon in half and stitch it to the top back seam about 2¹/₂ in (6 cm) down from the fold. Tie the loose ends in a neat bow.

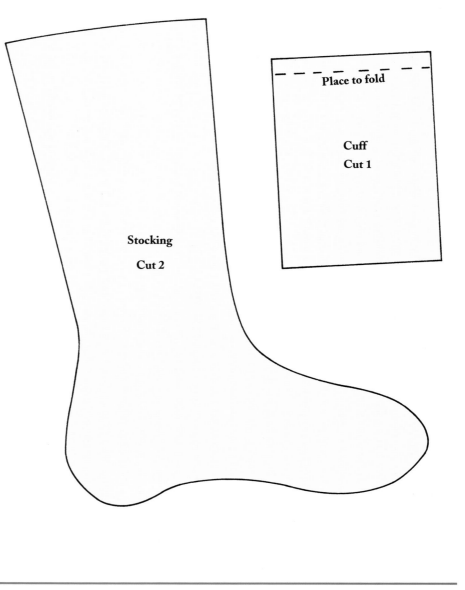

Stocking

Cut 2

Place to fold

Cuff

Cut 1

Christmas Cherub

This pretty cherub makes a charming Christmas tree decoration.
As with the other felt tree decorations, only simple stitching is required
– and if you prefer, you could glue on the decorations.

BELOW: *The blue–green net used for the skirt and wings is a subtle, understated colour combination, but the sequins on the wings and hair give the necessary touch of glamour.*

MATERIALS

6 x 4 in (15 x 10 cm) piece of pale pink felt
•
Matching thread
•
Doll's hair
•
2 blue beads for eyes
•
Red embroidery thread
•
3 red sequins

12 x 2 in (30 x 5 cm) length of pale or medium-toned net
•
24 x 2 in (45 x 5 cm) length of darker net
•
10 silver or gold sequins
•
18-in (45-cm) length of ribbon, 1/4 in (6 mm) wide

1 Cut out two body pieces from pale pink felt, using the template opposite. Sew the pieces together, keeping as close to the outer edge as possible. Tie off any loose threads.

2 Arrange the doll's hair neatly around the back of the head and hand stitch in place at the top and sides, taking care to stitch through only one layer of fabric.

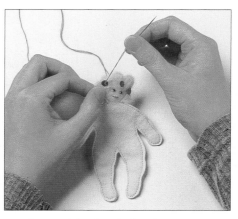

3 Sew on blue beads for the eyes, stitch the mouth in red embroidery thread, and add three red sequins to the front of the cherub's hair.

4 To make the skirt, cut a 12 x 2 in (30 x 5 cm) piece of net from each colour. Place one piece of net on top of the other and tack along one long edge.

5 Cut two left and two right wings from the remaining darker shade of net, using the templates opposite. Stitch together in pairs and decorate with silver or gold sequins.

**Left wing
Cut 2**

**Cherub
Cut 2**

**Right wing
Cut 2**

BELOW: *The skirt and wings on these cherubs are made from contrasting, but complementary, colours. Experiment with your own favourite colour combinations, but remember that this design generally works best if you use one pale and one darker tone of net.*

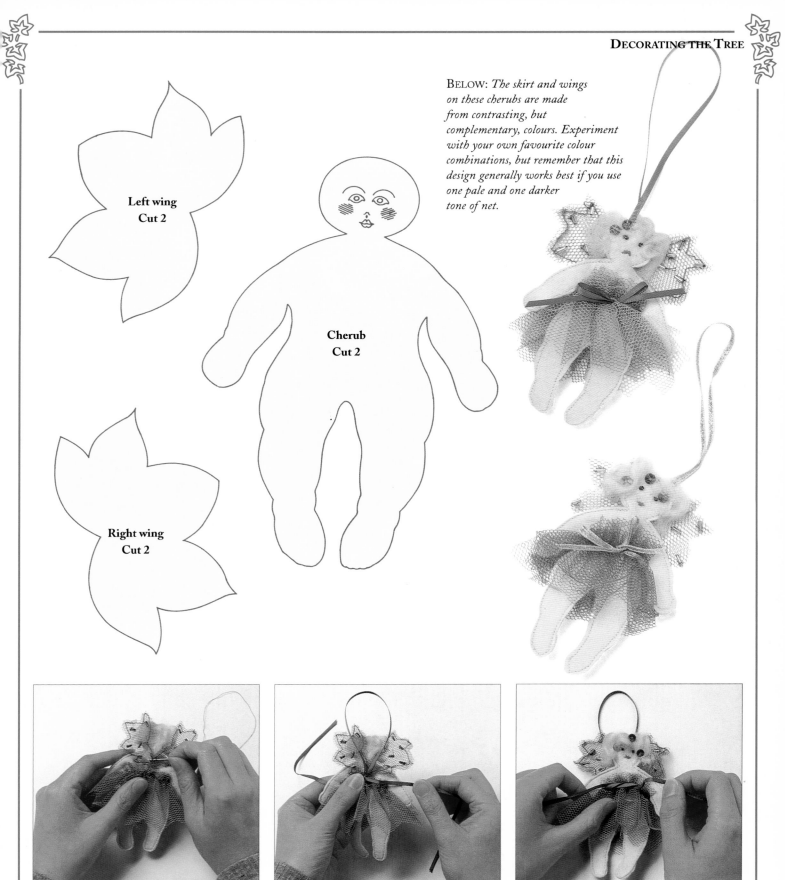

6 Place the skirt on the cherub and pull the tacking threads to gather evenly. Stitch to the body. Overlap the wings at the base and stitch to the cherub's back.

7 Fold the ribbon in half and stitch to the centre back about 3 in (7.5 cm) down from the fold.

8 Bring the loose ends of ribbon around to the front of the cherub and tie in a neat bow to form a sash. Cut off any excess ribbon on the diagonal.

Scented Sachets

These tiny sachets are filled with dried lavender flowerheads and can be decorated with any of the cross-stitch motifs on pages 52–53.

MATERIALS

For one sachet:

10-count Aida fabric
•
Embroidery thread
•
Muslin
•
Dried lavender flowerheads
•
12-in (30-cm) length of ribbon,
$\frac{1}{4}$ in (2.5 mm) wide, for trimming

Tiny beads for decoration
•
14-in (35-cm) length of ribbon,
$\frac{1}{4}$ in (5 mm) wide, for loop
•
7-in (17.5-cm) length of ribbon,
$\frac{1}{4}$ in (5 mm) wide, for bow

BELOW: *A snowflake embroidered in white stands out best on a dark fabric such as this mossy green. If your fabric is a dark colour, it usually looks best if the ribbon loop and bow are in the same shade.*

1 Cross stitch your chosen motif into the middle of a $2\frac{1}{2}$-in (6-cm) square of 10-count Aida fabric. Stitch around the edges to prevent fraying. Sew on beads if desired. Tie off loose threads.

2 Turn over the raw edges of the Aida fabric and press with your fingertips to flatten them. Machine stitch in place and tie off loose threads.

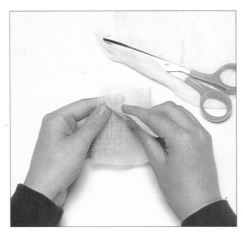

3 Cut a 6 x 3 in (15 x 7.5 cm) piece of muslin and fold it in half lengthways to form a square.

4 Stitch along three sides, leaving one end open. Turn inside out so that the stitches are on the inside and trim the open end to neaten.

5 Sew the muslin to the back of the cross-stitched motif, leaving the open end of the sachet unstitched. Fold under the raw edge of the muslin and press down with your fingertips.

6 Fill the sachet with dried lavender or any pot pourri of your choice and tack down the open edge of the sachet.

7 Machine stitch a ribbon border around all four sides of the front of the sachet, leaving a small loop in each corner, using ⅛-in (3-mm) ribbon. Stitch a bead into each corner.

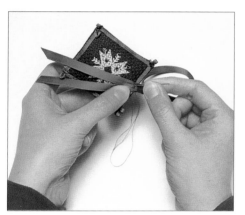

8 Take the long length of ribbon for the loop and fold it in half. Stitch to the front of the sachet about 2½-in (6 cm) down from the fold.

9 Place the short length of ribbon for the bow diagonally across the loop stitches and stitch in place, leaving equal lengths of ribbon on either side of the centre stitch.

10 Tie the short length of ribbon in a neat bow. Tie the loose ends of the ribbon loop in a second bow. Adjust so that the two bows lie diagonally across each other and trim to neaten.

CITRUS-SCENTED POT POURRI

On their own, dried lavender flowerheads have a powerful, heavy fragrance. If your taste leans towards something lighter, try this tangy, citrus-scented version. Vary the leaves to suit whatever is available from your garden and display any left-over pot pourri in a ceramic bowl, perhaps adding a few orange or yellow flowerheads, such as rose buds or marigolds, to make it look more attractive.

1 pint (500 ml) mixed scented leaves such as thyme, marjoram, rosemary, scented geranium or lemon balm

•

1 oz (25 g) orris root powder

•

1 oz (25 g) lavender flowerheads

•

Small pieces of orange, lemon or grapefruit peel

•

4-6 drops lemon oil

Mix all the ingredients together and leave in a cool, dark place for a few weeks before using.

Cross-Stitch Motifs

abcdefghijk

lmnopqrs

tuvwxyz

1234567890

Kumquat Pomanders

Pomanders have been used for hundreds, if not thousands, of years. In this version, tiny kumquats are spiked with cloves and left to dry in a spicy mix of cinnamon and allspice to provide a warm, wintery fragrance reminiscent of mulled wine.

RIGHT: *This pomander is a very natural-looking tree decoration; it could easily be mistaken for a tiny pine cone. Its subtle fragrance will last right through the Christmas period.*

MATERIALS

For each pomander:

Masking tape

•

1 kumquat

•

20-30 cloves

•

8-in (20-cm) length of ribbon, $\frac{1}{8}$ in (3 mm) wide

•

All-purpose glue

•

Ribbon curls to decorate (see page 127)

For the curing powder:

4 oz (125 g) cinnamon powder

•

4 oz (125 g) allspice

•

2 oz (50 g) orris root powder

1 Cut a narrow strip of masking tape and place it lengthways around the kumquat, overlapping the ends slightly and pressing down firmly to make sure it adheres to the fruit.

2 Using a nail or a wooden cocktail stick, prick holes in the kumquat on either side of the masking tape.

3 Push one clove into each hole.

4 Prick another series of holes lengthways around the kumquat at 90 degrees to the first. Push in cloves as before until the kumquat is covered.

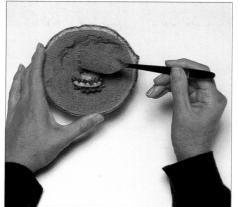

5 Place the kumquats in a bowl and cover completely with curing powder. Leave for 3–4 weeks, turning every few days so that they dry evenly.

6 Remove the kumquats from the curing powder and peel off the masking tape. Tie a length of ribbon around each kumquat in the gap left by the masking tape.

BELOW: *As the pomanders are not very colourful in their own right, use ribbons in a range of bright colours to make them stand out against the dark green of the tree. Make the ribbon loops longer than for most tree decorations so that they can be arranged to hang like tassels from the branches of the tree.*

7 Tie the loose ribbon ends together at the top to form a loop for hanging the pomander on the tree. Snip off any excess ribbon on the diagonal to neaten the loop.

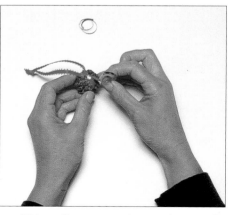

8 Using all-purpose glue, stick a couple of short ribbon curls (see page 127) to the pomander.

Christmas Cookies

Children will enjoy helping to decorate these Christmas cookies. The cookies should be eaten within a week of being made – though you probably won't be able to resist them for that long!

BASIC RECIPE

For the cookies:

3 oz (75 g) butter
•
1 1/2 oz (40 g) caster sugar
•
1 oz (25 g) cornflour
•
3 oz (75 g) plain flour

Pre-heat the oven to
gas mark 2, 300 °F (150 °C).
Cream together the butter and half the sugar
in a mixing bowl until light and fluffy, using a
wooden spoon.
Fold in the cornflour and flour, and then
the remaining sugar.
Press the mixture into a 7 x 10 in
(17.5 x 25 cm) baking tin. Cover with
greaseproof paper and a layer of dried beans
or lentils and bake blind for approximately
30 minutes.
Remove from the oven. When cool enough
to handle, cut into the desired shapes and
place on a cooling tray. Work quickly in
order to decorate the cookies before they
cool completely.

For the water icing:

8 oz (250 g) icing sugar
•
6 dessertspoons warm water

Mix together the icing sugar and water to
the consistency of pouring cream.

CHRISTMAS STARS

For the decoration:

Drinking straws
•
1 quantity water icing
•
Chocolate chips
•
Silver cake decorations
•
8-in (20-cm) lengths of ribbon,
$^1/_4$ in (6 mm) wide

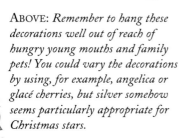

ABOVE: *Remember to hang these decorations well out of reach of hungry young mouths and family pets! You could vary the decorations by using, for example, angelica or glacé cherries, but silver somehow seems particularly appropriate for Christmas stars.*

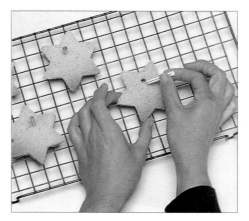

1 Push a short length of a drinking
straw into the top of each cookie
shape to make a hole for hanging. Leave
the straw in place.

2 Using a palette knife, put a small
amount of water icing in the middle
of each shape. Working quickly before the
cookies cool, spread the icing evenly over
the top and sides.

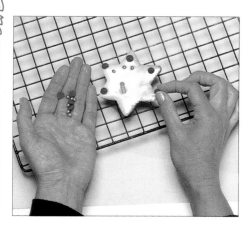

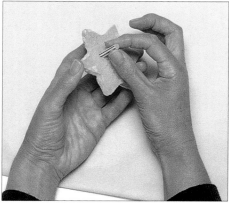

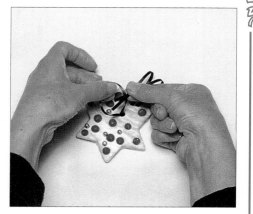

3 Decorate the cookies with chocolate chips and silver cake decorations. Leave to cool. Store in an airtight container for two days to allow the icing to harden.

4 Remove the drinking straws by pushing them through the back of the cookies from the front. (If you pull out the straws from the front, you may crack the icing.)

5 Fold a ribbon length in half and push the folded end through the hole in the cookie from the back. Feed the cut ends through the loop and pull tight.

6 Tie the cut ends together to form a loop for hanging and cut off any excess ribbon on the diagonal to neaten.

LEFT AND ABOVE: *Cookie cutters are available in a wide range of shapes. Here, heart-shaped cookies are decorated with candied fruits on melted chocolate and multi-coloured cake decorations on glistening white water icing.*

MATERIALS

For the decoration:

1 quantity water icing

•

Silver cake decorations

•

Angelica

•

Chocolate chips

•

Desiccated coconut

•

Marzipan

•

Red and green food colouring

•

8-in (20-cm) lengths of ribbon,
¼ in (6 mm) wide

1 Cut out snowmen shapes and cover the top and sides with water icing. Add the eyes (silver cake decorations), mouth (angelica) and buttons (chocolate chips). Sprinkle with desiccated coconut.

2 Add drops of red food colouring to a small piece of marzipan and blend until the colour is evenly distributed. Colour another piece of marzipan green in the same way.

LEFT: *The Snowman Cookie is dressed in a jolly red-and-green scarf, and the desiccated coconut covering is ideal for giving the impression of crisp, textured winter snow.*

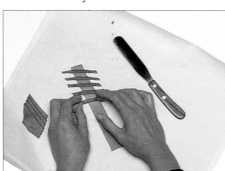

3 Roll out the green marzipan and cut a 6 x ½ in (15 x 1.5 cm) rectangle for the scarf. Place tiny strips of red marzipan diagonally on it, pressing down firmly.

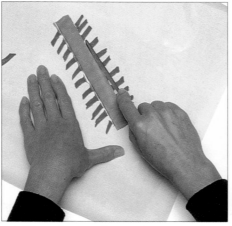

4 Turn the marzipan strip over and trim off the excess red marzipan.

5 Place the scarf around the snowman's neck and cross the ends over at the front. Press gently to secure, and tie a ribbon loop (see Christmas Star recipe, steps 5 and 6).

Cotton Snowballs

*To make these snowballs, spray a little gold (or silver) paint onto the
leaves and add a decorative ribbon. The shiny metallic paint
perfectly complements the fluffiness of the cotton.*

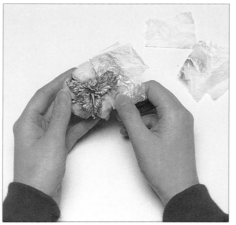

ABOVE: *A boldly coloured red
ribbon provides a dramatic
contrast to the gold and white of
the cotton ball.*

1 Detach the cotton ball from its
branch, leaving a 2-in (5-cm) stalk
attached.

2 Place tissue paper under the leaves to
keep the cotton ball clean and spray
the leaves with gold paint. Leave to dry,
then carefully remove the protective
tissue paper.

MATERIALS

Natural cotton ball with stalk attached
(available from dried flower suppliers)

•

Tissue paper

•

Gold spray paint

•

10-in (25-cm) length of ribbon, 1/4 in
(6 mm) wide

3 Fold the ribbon in half, secure with a
stitch approximately 2 1/2 in (6 cm)
from the fold and tie it around the stalk.

4 Cut off any excess ribbon and fluff
up the cotton ball to a neat shape.

LEFT: *Using the same colour for
both the leaves and the ribbon
(here gold on gold and silver on
silver) offers a more subtle
and restrained colour
combination.*

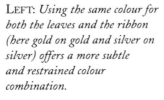

Dried Apple Sprays

*Most of the ingredients in these dried apple sprays can easily be found
around the home and garden. Quick and easy to produce, they make a very
effective and natural-looking tree or parcel decoration.*

MATERIALS

For each spray:

Florist's reel wire

•

2 dried apple slices (see page 127)

•

3 artificial red berries with stems

•

3–4 sprigs of small leaves (e.g., privet), sprayed gold, 5 in (12.5 cm) long

•

Thin gold ribbon or twine, 4 in (10 cm) long

•

All-purpose clear adhesive

•

2 small gold ribbon curls (see page 127)

•

20-in (50-cm) length of wired blue-green chiffon ribbon,

LEFT: *Restraint is the key to
the success of this decoration. There is
only a hint of red in the apple
slices and tiny berries, but it provides
a very effective contrast to the
muted blue-green and gold used
elsewhere. The gold paint on the
leaves is applied very lightly so that
some green is still visible, and this hint
of green helps to give the decoration
a very natural feel.*

1 Thread a 6-in (15-cm) length of florist's reel wire through
the needle holes in the apple slices, leaving an equal amount
of wire on each side. Twist the wires together.

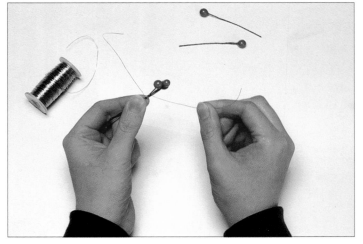

2 Take three artificial berries and wrap reel wire around their
stems to wire them into a bunch. Leave about 3 in (7.5 cm)
of wire protruding.

3 Place the berries on top of the apple slices, holding the berry stems and apple wires in one hand. Wrap reel wire around the berry stems and apple wires to bind them together.

4 Place the leaf sprigs behind the apples and berries. Hold a gold twine loop behind the leaves. Use the reel wire from the berries to bind everything together.

5 Place two tiny dabs of glue on the front of the spray and press on the ribbon curls. Leave to dry.

6 Tie a wired blue-green chiffon ribbon bow around the top of the spray, taking care to hide the stalks and wire. Trim the ribbon ends on the diagonal to tidy.

LEFT: *Apple skins come in many different colours, from bright red to pure, deep green with wonderfully patterned combinations of these colours in between. They can look very dramatic when several colours are combined in an arrangement or decoration. For instructions on how to make dried apple slices, see page 127.*

Twig & Berry Bunches

You can find most of the ingredients for these twig and berry bunches in your own garden. The ribbon bows and curls, which can be made from any brightly coloured leftover scraps, provide a very effective contrast to the natural ingredients.

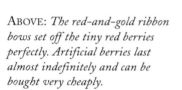

ABOVE: *The red-and-gold ribbon bows set off the tiny red berries perfectly. Artificial berries last almost indefinitely and can be bought very cheaply.*

MATERIALS

For each bunch:

12 thin birch twigs, 4 in (10 cm) long

•

Reel wire

•

All-purpose clear adhesive

•

2 sprigs of small leaves sprayed silver and gold

•

5 sprigs of artificial berries

•

5-in (12.5-cm) length of green ribbon, ³⁄₄ in (2 cm) wide

•

Two 9-in (22.5-cm) lengths of red-and-gold ribbon, ¹⁄₄ in (6 mm) wide

•

8-in (20-cm) length of green ribbon for loop, ³⁄₄ in (2 cm) wide

1 Spray half the birch twigs silvery-white and leave the others plain. Make them into a bunch and twist a short piece of reel wire around the middle to secure.

2 Dab glue onto the middle of the twig bunch. Press on the leaf sprigs with their stalks overlappping in the middle. Hold them in position until they are firmly stuck in place.

3 Glue on the sprigs of artificial berries in the same way, placing three on one end of the bunch and two on the other.

RIGHT: *A double silver ribbon bow picks up the silvery-white colour of some of the birch twigs, while the red loop echoes the colour of the berries.*

LEFT: *Fine silver twigs are tied together with a silver ribbon bow to form a fan-shaped spray. The remaining ingredients – tiny gold pine cones, oak leaves, and silver ribbon curls (see page 127) – are then glued onto the spray to complete the decoration.*

RIGHT: *A spray of brown and gold leaves, with a few artificial berries for extra colour, is tied with a decorative gold ribbon. A gold loop and red ribbon curls provide the finishing touches.*

4 Tie the 5-in (12.5-cm) length of green ribbon once around the middle of the bunch to hide the overlapping stalks. Trim the ends on the diagonal to neaten.

5 Tie one red-and-gold ribbon around the bunch in a bow. Thread the second ribbon through the bow at a diagonal to the first and tie in a bow.

6 Fold the 8-in (20-cm) length of green ribbon in half to form a loop and stitch it onto the wide ribbon at the back of the twig bunch.

Lucky Dip Tree Tub

*Although a lot of effort goes into creating Christmas tree decorations,
the base of the tree is often overlooked. This Lucky Dip Tree Tub
provides a novel solution. Children will love it – especially when they
discover the presents hidden in the wood shavings!*

MATERIALS

1 wooden plant container, at least 6 in (15 cm) larger than the
Christmas tree container, sprayed gold

•

Gold-and-silver ribbon, $\frac{1}{2}$ in (12 mm) wide

•

A selection of small presents

•

A selection of lollipops and other candy sticks

•

All-purpose glue

Lengths of red parcel ribbon, $\frac{1}{2}$ in (12 mm) wide, the same
length as the depth of the tub

•

Lengths of red parcel ribbon, $\frac{1}{4}$ in (6 mm) wide, 3 in (7.5 cm)
shorter than the depth of the tub

•

Lengths of green parcel ribbon, $\frac{1}{4}$ in (3 mm) wide, $1\frac{1}{2}$ times the
depth of the tub

•

Wood shavings, sprayed gold and silver

LEFT: *Make sure that your
Christmas tree is securely wedged
in place so that there is no risk of
it toppling over. Plant it in its
own container and then put the*
*container inside the tub. Pack
earth firmly around the tree
container, stopping about 3 in
(7.5 cm) from the rim, and fill the
tub with wood shavings.*

1 Take a small, cellophane-wrapped candy stick and, using gold and silver ribbon, tie a bow around one end. Trim off the ends of the ribbon to neaten.

2 Take another piece of the same ribbon measuring the depth of the tub plus at least 4 in (10 cm). Glue it to the back of the ribbon bow that you tied around the candy stick.

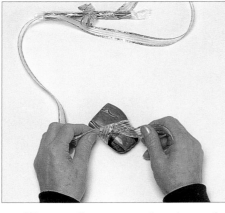

ABOVE: *Soft toys such as this cuddly hedgehog are always popular with young children and you can buy – or even make – them at very little cost. Dolls, dolls' house furniture, wooden animals or cars, small diaries: all these would be suitable. The important thing is to get things that are small enough to be completely hidden in the wood shavings.*

3 Wind the ribbon diagonally around the candy stick and secure at the top with a dab of glue, pressing firmly to fix in place. Do not cut off the excess ribbon.

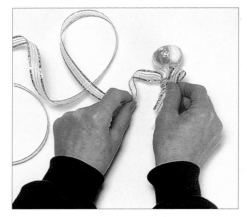

4 Tie a small present to the other end of the ribbon and trim the ends to neaten.

5 Take another length of gold-and-silver ribbon measuring the depth of the tub plus at least 4 in (10 cm) and tie a bow around a lollipop stick, just under the lollipop.

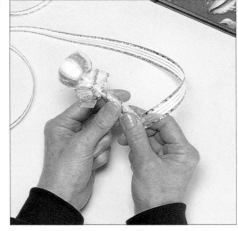

6 Wind the ribbon diagonally around the lollipop stick and secure it at the base with a dab of glue, pressing firmly to fix it in place. Do not cut off the excess ribbon.

7 Tie a small present to the other end of the ribbon and trim the ends on the diagonal to neaten.

8 Curl the wide red parcel ribbon lengths by running the edge of a pair of scissors along them (see page 127).

9 Glue the ribbon curls to the top of the tub so that they cover the join between alternate panels.

10 Curl the narrow red ribbon lengths in the same way and glue them to the top of the tub to cover the joins between the remaining panels.

11 Curl the narrow green ribbon lengths, fold each one in half, and glue one on top of each length of narrow red ribbon.

LEFT: Woodworkers' workshops are always littered with shavings that get swept up and thrown away at the end of the day. Save them and spray them gold and silver for use in this imaginative Lucky Dip Tree Tub.

12 Tuck the presents into the wood shavings between the edge of the tub and the Christmas tree container. The candy sticks and lollipops hang down on the outside of the tub.

Terracotta Tree Pot

This painted terracotta pot, with its swags of crisp white net and glittering silver star and ribbons, is a stylish yet very simple Christmas tree container.

LEFT: *Apart from the white and silver of the swag, everything else in this project is in varying shades of green – and this allows the rim decoration to stand out all the more spectacularly.*

MATERIALS

Terracotta plant pot and saucer (size depends on the size of your tree)

•

Household emulsion paint

•

1 yd (1 m) white net, 4 times the diameter of the pot in length

•

9 strips of white net, 1 x 12 in (2.5 x 30 cm)

•

8 lengths of silver ribbon, 1 x 10 in (2.5 x 25 cm)

•

Glue gun

•

All-purpose glue

•

Silver star, at least 4 in (20 cm) from top to bottom

•

Lichen moss

•

Green glass nuggets

1 Paint the terracotta pot and saucer in the colour of your choice, using ordinary household emulsion paint. When the paint is dry, mark eight equal intervals around the rim of the pot.

2 Divide the main piece of net into eight equal sections along its length by tying one small net strip around the main piece at the starting point of each division.

3 Tie the final net strip around the loose end of the swag. With a sharp pair of scissors, cut off the excess net from the strips.

4 Turn the net swag over so that the knots on the strips are at the back. Tie a length of silver ribbon over the net strips, starting with the second net strip and ending with the eighth.

5 Trim the ends of the silver ribbon on the diagonal to about 2 in (5 cm) in length.

6 Using a glue gun, start gluing the net swag to the rim of the pot, matching each ribbon to one of the points marked on the pot in step 1.

ABOVE: *Strips of silver ribbon tied around the net swag echo the colour and sparkle of the star without dominating it.*

RIGHT: *Deep green lichen moss and glass nuggets in two different shades provide the finishing touches.*

7 Continue until you have attached the swag to seven of the points marked around the rim.

8 Put a small dab of glue on each end of the net swag and press them firmly together to secure.

9 Tie the last piece of silver ribbon around the glued ends of the swag to hide the join. Dab glue onto the pot at the last marked point and press the swag onto the pot.

10 Glue the silver star decoration to the middle of one of the silver ribbons. The star should stick up slightly above the rim of the pot.

11 When you have planted your Christmas tree in the pot and secured it firmly with soil or sand, cover the top of the soil with lichen moss to keep in the moisture.

12 To add sparkle to the base of the pot, fill the saucer with glass nuggets in two shades of green.

DECORATING THE TABLE

*C*hristmas is a time for reunion, with family and friends coming together in celebration. A special Christmas meal is an integral part of the celebrations, yet however good a cook you are, the food is only part of the story. A well decorated table can turn even the most ordinary meal into an occasion to remember, with candles, cut-glass crystal and fine china all contributing to the festive atmosphere.

This chapter demonstrates two elegant and easy-to-make table linen sets that will complement all styles of table decoration. The quilted place mats on pages 72–77 would look superb on any type of plain wooden table, from country pine to antique oak or mahogany, their brightly patterned ribbon border allowing them to stand out boldly against the grain of waxed and polished wood. The damask table cloth and napkins on pages 78–81, with their sophisticated appliqué motifs of seasonal flora, can be adapted to incorporate any Christmas motifs of your choice and to fit any size of table. Stunning and stylish, both designs are sufficiently timeless to be brought out year after year, becoming treasured parts of your family Christmas. They would make wonderful gifts; you could also adapt the idea to incorporate non-Christmas motifs, thus transforming the most workaday piece of table linen into a unique design of your own.

To give a focal point to your table decorations, this chapter also includes instructions for two floral centrepieces – a sumptous-looking arrangement with gold candles and vibrant red poinsettias that is perfect for a formal dinner party, and a more traditional-looking display using the perenially popular combination of holly and ivy. Both these designs could be scaled down in size to make miniature versions to set beside individual place settings.

LEFT: *The golden candles in the centrepiece perfectly complement the rich colours of the table linen – perfect proof of the fact that you don't have to spend a fortune to create elegant and stylish table settings.*

Quilted Place Mats

*These festive green and red chintz place mats look so pretty that
it's a shame to hide them under a plate! The complete setting
consists of place mats, a striking diamond-shaped table
runner, napkins and napkin rings.*

ABOVE: *Red and green is always a
strong colour combination. This
wide ribbon border, with its rich
mix of colours, makes a bold
colour statement when arranged on
the table.*

MATERIALS

For each mat:

10¼-in (26-cm) square of washable interfacing

•

10¼-in (26-cm) square of green cotton

•

17¾-in (45-cm) square of red chintz

•

½ yd (50 cm) of Christmas ribbon, 3 in (7.5 cm) wide

•

Matching thread

1 Place the interfacing on top of the green cotton. Tack around the edges to join the two pieces of fabric together.

2 Place the red chintz right side down and fold in 3⁵/₈ in (6.5 cm) on all four sides. Press each side with an iron to leave a bold crease line.

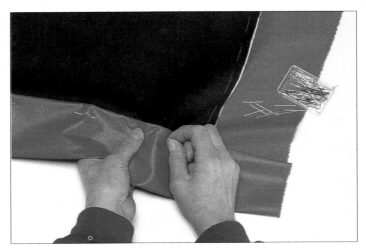

3 Open out and place the green cotton and interfacing inside the crease lines. Turn under the raw edge of the chintz by ⁵/₈ in (1.5 cm) to give a 3-in (7.5-cm) border. Pin to hold.

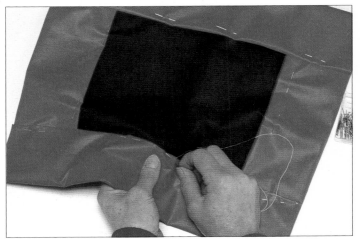

4 Tack around the pin lines, keeping close to the edge and making sure that you stitch through all three fabric layers.

5 Lay the Christmas ribbon along one side of the red border so that an equal amount of red chintz is visible above and below the ribbon. Pin in place.

LEFT: *This seasonal pattern of pine cones, holly leaves and apples, makes a bright, decorative border.*

6 Form a neat mitred corner by folding the ribbon up at a right angle and then laying it along the adjoining side of the mat. Pin in place.

7 At the final corner, cut off the excess ribbon to align with the edge of the ribbon border on the adjoining side.

8 Fold the corner in at a right angle to form the last mitre and pin in place.

9 Tack along the inner and outer edges of the ribbon border and along the mitred corners, keeping about ¼ in (6 mm) from the edge of the ribbon. Remove the pins as you go.

10 Machine stitch the ribbon border in place, keeping as close as possible to the edge of the ribbon. Remove the tacking stitches. Press.

TABLE RUNNER

MATERIALS

Make two small squares, following the instructions on pages 72–74, and one large square using the amounts below:

$20^1/_4$-in (51.5-cm) square of red chintz

•

$12^3/_4$-in (22.5-cm) square of green cotton

•

$12^3/_4$-in (22.5-cm) square of interfacing

52 in (132 cm) Christmas ribbon, 3 in (7.5 cm) wide

•

Matching thread

RIGHT: *This bold triple diamond table runner comprises one large and two small squares, made in the same way as the place mats on pages 72–74 and then joined together.*

1 Overlap the large square on top of the small squares in a diamond formation, leaving $1^1/_2$ in (4 cm) of green cotton visible on all the small squares. Pin and tack the squares together.

2 To join all three squares together, machine stitch around all edges where the large and small square overlap and along the mitred corners of the ribbon border on the large square.

NAPKINS & NAPKIN RINGS

MATERIALS

For each napkin:

12-in (30-cm) square of dark green cotton

•

Matching thread

For each napkin ring:

4½ x 7½ in (11.5 x 19 cm) piece
of red chintz

3 x 7 in (7.5 x 17.5 cm) piece
of interfacing

•

7½-in (19-cm) length of Christmas ribbon,
3 in (7.5 cm) wide

•

Matching thread

ABOVE: *The napkin is made
from the same dark green cotton
that was used in the centre
of the place mats, setting off the
rich red contained in the
napkin ring.*

1 To make the napkins, turn under the raw edges of the fabric square by pressing with your fingertips and fold over again. Tack to hold in place and machine stitch around all four edges.

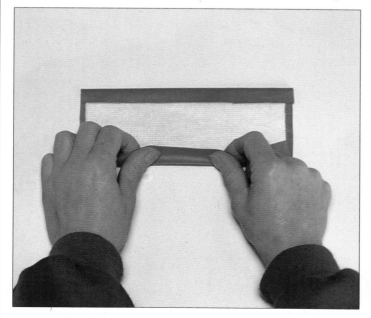

2 To make the napkin rings, place the red chintz right side down and place the interfacing on top of it. Fold over the edges of the chintz and press in place.

3 Place the Christmas ribbon on top of the chintz, with an equal amount of red chintz showing top and bottom of the ribbon, and pin and tack in place.

4 Machine stitch down both sides of the ribbon, keeping as close to the edge as you can.

5 Fold the napkin ring in half with the ribbon on the inside. Tack across the short end about $^3/_8$ in (1 cm) in from the outer edge.

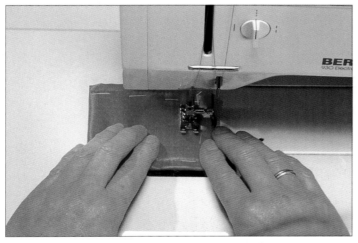

6 Machine stitch across the short end about $^5/_8$ in (1.5 cm) from the end.

7 Remove the tacking stitches. Carefully trim one seam on the short end of the napkin ring to within about $^1/_4$ in (6 mm) of the machine stitches.

8 Fold the untrimmed seam over the trimmed seam, turning the raw edge under, and pin in place. Slipstitch neatly along this edge.

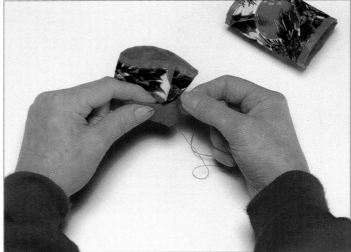

9 Turn the napkin ring right side out and neatly oversew each seam end. Pull the napkin ring into shape to finish.

Appliqué Tablecloth

Appliqué artistry! This elegant Christmas table linen set of poinsettias, roses and pine cones appliquéd onto a crisp damask cloth and napkins is something that you will want to use year after year.

MAKING THE CLOTH

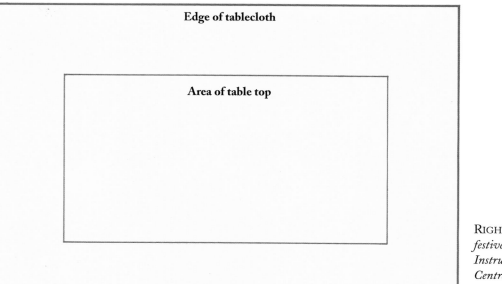

Edge of tablecloth

Area of table top

MATERIALS

Damask table cloth and napkins
•
Printed Christmas fabric
•
Matching thread

RIGHT: *A table for two with a festive border of Christmas flora. Instructions for the Holly and Ivy Centrepiece are given on pages 85–87.*

1 Place the cloth on the table, with an equal amount overhanging each side. Tack around the table-top area to give yourself a guide to where to position the appliqué motifs.

LEFT: *The motif for the corners of the tablecloth. Use large, bold designs and always wash the printed fabric before you cut out the motifs to check that it is colour fast.*

2 Cut out motifs from Christmas fabric. Choose fabric with large motifs: small designs are fiddly to work with and they will lack impact when seen from a distance.

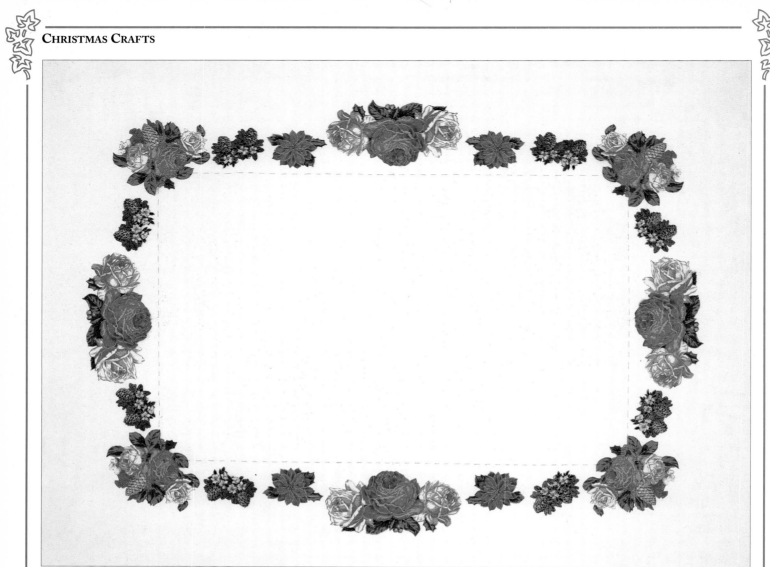

3 Lay the cloth out flat and mark the centre of each side. Pin on the motifs, using the tacking stitches as a guide. Space the motifs evenly and symmetrically around the cloth.

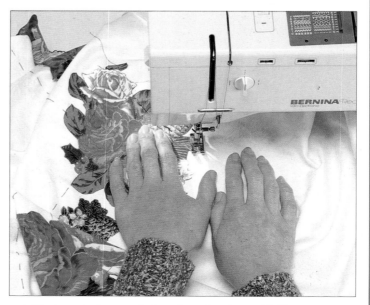

4 Tack each motif in place, tacking at least $\frac{1}{2}$ in (1 cm) in from the edge. Remove the pins.

5 Zigzag stitch around the edge of each motif. Choose a thread colour that matches the motifs and contrasts with the table cloth to give a crisp edge to the appliqué work.

MAKING THE NAPKINS

1 Carefully cut out a motif large enough to fit comfortably in one corner of the napkin. In this case, two contrasting pieces have been selected.

2 Pin the two motifs together, making sure they are identical for each napkin. You may need to try several combinations before you find a satisfactory arrangement.

3 Pin the completed design to one corner of the napkin and tack to hold the motif firmly in place.

4 Zigzag stitch around the edge of the motif in the same way as for making the tablecloth.

ABOVE: *The bold red stitching around the edge of the motif stands out well against the crisp white damask.*

Golden Candle Centrepiece

This is an elegant and seasonal centrepiece for a formal Christmas dinner party. The red poinsettias in the centre of the arrangement provide a vibrant splash of seasonal colour.

MATERIALS

10-in (25-cm) wreath base of artificial pine

Lengths of artificial grape vine with berries

Fine reel wire

4 artificial white roses

4 sprigs of artificial rose leaves, sprayed gold

All-purpose glue

Eight 4-in (10-cm) gold candles, $1/2$ in (1 cm) in diameter

Eight $1/2$-in (1-cm) candle holders

8-in (20-cm) plate or shallow dish

3–4 fresh miniature poinsettias

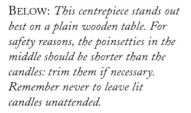

BELOW: *This centrepiece stands out best on a plain wooden table. For safety reasons, the poinsetties in the middle should be shorter than the candles: trim them if necessary. Remember never to leave lit candles unattended.*

1 Re-shape the artificial wreath base if necessary in order to form a true circle. The success of this arrangement depends on perfect symmetry.

2 Bend each sprig of artificial grape vine to follow the shape of the wreath base and arrange the leaves and berries attractively.

BELOW: *These artificial white roses stand out well against the rich, dark colours of the wreath base. The gold-sprayed leaves will pick up the glow of the candlelight.*

3 Lay the grape vine on top of the wreath base and fix it in place by wrapping fine reel wire around the vine and base. Twist the wires together on the underside of the wreath.

4 Join each white rose to a sprig of gold-sprayed rose leaves by twisting their stems firmly together.

5 Space the four roses evenly around the wreath and wire them in place by wrapping fine reel wire over the stems and around the wreath base.

6 Work around the wreath, adjusting the grape vine leaves so that they cover the reel wire as much as possible.

7 Put a dab of strong, all-purpose glue on each candle holder and press the candle onto it, holding it for a few moments to secure. Make sure the candle is vertical.

8 Distribute the candles around the wreath, making sure that they are evenly spaced.

9 When you are satisfied that the candles are correctly positioned, glue them in place. Hold until secure, making sure they are truly vertical.

10 Place the wreath over a plate and put 3–4 pots of miniature poinsettias in the centre, making sure that the plate is completely hidden.

Holly & Ivy Centrepiece

*This beautifully rounded centrepiece uses the contrast of variegated ivy
against dark green holly and ivy leaves to great effect. Tiny gold leaves and
bright red berries add a subtle touch of warmth.*

ABOVE: *The exact positioning
of the leaves and berries is not
important but avoid having clusters
of the same sort of foliage close
together. The centrepiece should last
for at least 10 days, but add
a little more water to the oasis
if the foliage starts to wilt.*

MATERIALS

4¹/₂-in (12-cm) square of thick cardboard

•

5-in (12.5-cm) square of plastic, cut
from a bin liner

•

All-purpose glue

•

4¹/₂-in (12-cm) square of pre-soaked oasis,
3 in (7.5 cm) deep

•

12 sprigs dark green holly (*Ilex* sp.)

12 sprigs dark green ivy with berries
(*Hedera* sp.)

•

12 sprigs variegated ivy (*Hedera* sp.)

•

6 sprigs small leaves such as oak or privet,
sprayed gold

•

6 sprigs large red berries (artificial)

•

6 sprigs small red berries (artificial)

ABOVE: *Small privet leaves sprayed gold on both sides. Along with the yellowy-gold of the variegated ivy leaves, these provide dramatic contrast to the dark green of the remaining foliage and help to 'lift' the arrangement.*

BELOW: *Artificial red berries can be positioned exactly where required for a jewel-like burst of colour.*

1 Coat one side of the square of cardboard with a thin layer of glue, and place the plastic square on top. This provides a waterproof base for the arrangement.

2 Turn the cardboard square over and fold in the edges of the plastic covering. Secure firmly along all four sides with strips of sticky tape.

3 Stand the pre-soaked oasis on the plastic-covered cardboard. Push sprigs of holly and each type of ivy into the top of the oasis, positioning them randomly.

4 Continue until the top of the oasis block is evenly covered in greenery. You will need about three sprigs of holly and three of each type of ivy to cover the top of the oasis completely.

5 Start adding holly and ivy to the sides of the oasis block, using approximately the same number of sprigs of foliage on each side.

6 Continue until the entire oasis block is evenly covered in greenery. Turn the arrangement as you work to check that each side looks balanced and rounded.

7 Space the gold leaves around the arrangement. Perfect symmetry is impossible as the sprigs are all slightly different in shape and size: aim for random splashes of sparkling gold.

8 Insert the sprigs of large and small red berries into the arrangement in the same way for a final touch of colour.

DECORATING THE HOME

For children and adults alike, Christmas is a time to fill the house with special decorations and this chapter contains a wide range of decorative ideas to suit all tastes.

No Christmas would be complete without a nativity scene to remind us of the miracle of the Holy birth, and this chapter includes a charming nativity sampler worked in cross stitch that you can pass down through your family for generations to come. If your taste leans towards traditional-style decorations, a wreath to welcome visitors to your door over the festive period is a must for any home, as are capacious stockings for the children to hang by the mantelpiece or at the foot of their bed until Father Christmas arrives. Father Christmas himself makes an appearance in this chapter, in the form of a colourful felt doll. Natural-looking Christmas decorations are always popular, and this chapter includes imaginative designs for a fireplace garland and matching log basket that will echo the warm glow of your fireside on a cold winter evening. Still on a natural theme, an unusual Christmas card holder made from trailing strands of dark green ivy shows just how easy it is to create an original and highly practical decoration from ingredients you can readily find in your own garden on on your favourite contry walk. Finally, two contrasting decorations for those of us with small apartments who don't want to miss out on the festivities by not having a traditional-style Christmas tree – a citrus-scented tree laden with colourful fruits and berries, and a vibrant orange and gold arrangement of honesty and Chinese lanterns.

This chapter has something for everyone. Fill your home with colour and fun and the spirit of Christmas. Create your own style. Above all, have fun!

LEFT: The fireside, stylishly decorated here by means of a colourful garland and matching log basket, is the focal point of any family home. Easy-to-make felt decorations (stockings and a delightful Father Christmas doll) add a youthful, colourful touch.

Nativity Sampler

This charming nativity scene would make a wonderful present — something to treasure and display every year. You could embroider your own special message using the alphabet chart provided here.

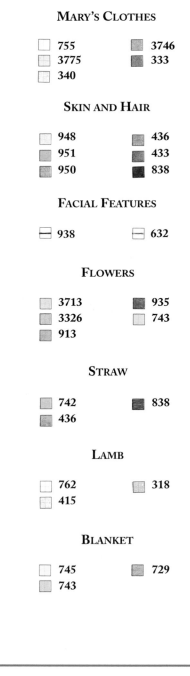

LEFT: Gold and silver threads enhance the sampler. Gold thread was used to outline the four crosses in the border. Gold was mixed with brown in Joseph's coat and silver added to the pale blue in Mary's veil.

MARY'S CLOTHES

☐	755	▨	3746
☐	3775	▨	333
☐	340		

SKIN AND HAIR

☐	948	▨	436
▨	951	▨	433
▨	950	■	838

FACIAL FEATURES

⊟	938	⊟	632

FLOWERS

☐	3713	▨	935
▨	3326	☐	743
▨	913		

STRAW

▨	742	▨	838
▨	436		

LAMB

☐	762	▨	318
☐	415		

BLANKET

☐	745	▨	729
☐	743		

MATERIALS

Finished size: 10½ x 8¼ in (260 x 208 mm)

15 x 13 in (360 x 310 mm) piece of 28-count Linda cloth, antique white

•

DMC stranded cotton, 1 skein of each colour listed

WORKING THE SAMPLER

Following the chart opposite, work the sampler in cross stitch over two strands of fabric using two strands of thread. Outline the figures in back stitch, using one strand of dark brown thread. You can substitute another make of thread if you prefer.

BORDER, ALPHABET AND DATE

☐	742	▨	3346
■	816	▨	791
☐	3348		

JOSEPH'S CLOTHES

▨	644	▨	976
▨	647	▨	420
▨	840		
■	838		
▨	842		
▨	3787		

Chart for the Nativity Sampler

Father Christmas Doll

*This colourful Father Christmas doll is full of character and will
be adored by children and adults alike. Made from brightly coloured
felt, it will brighten up any shelf or mantelpiece.*

MATERIALS

12-in (30-cm) square of pink/flesh-coloured
felt

•

12-in (30-cm) squares of red felt

•

10-in (25-cm) square of brown felt

•

10-in (25-cm) square of white felt

•

Kapok

•

Fabric glue

•

Cotton wool for the hair, beard and
moustache

•

Circles of white, blue and red felt for the eyes
and mouth

•

White bobble for hat

ABOVE: *The Father Christmas
doll shown here is about 11 in
(27.5 cm) tall. You could make a
larger version by enlarging
the templates on a photocopier:
simply increase them all by the
same percentage.*

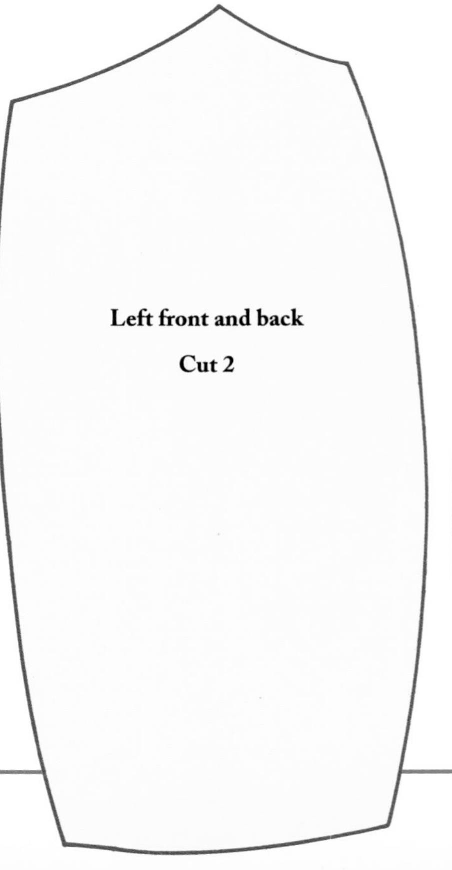

Left front and back

Cut 2

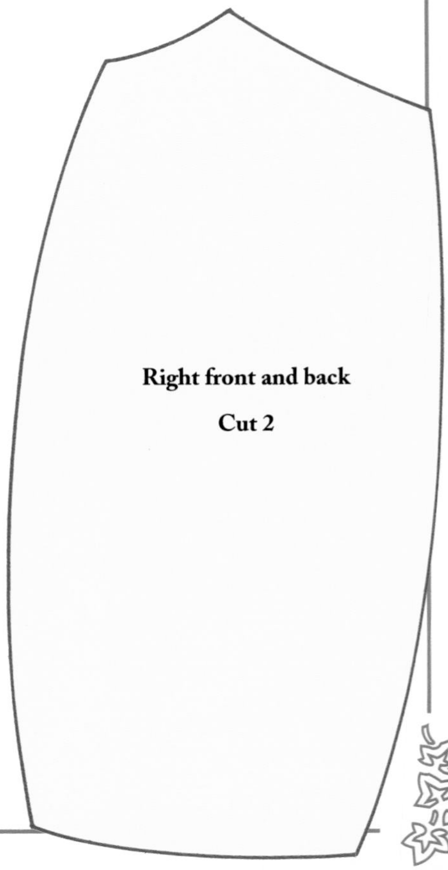

Right front and back

Cut 2

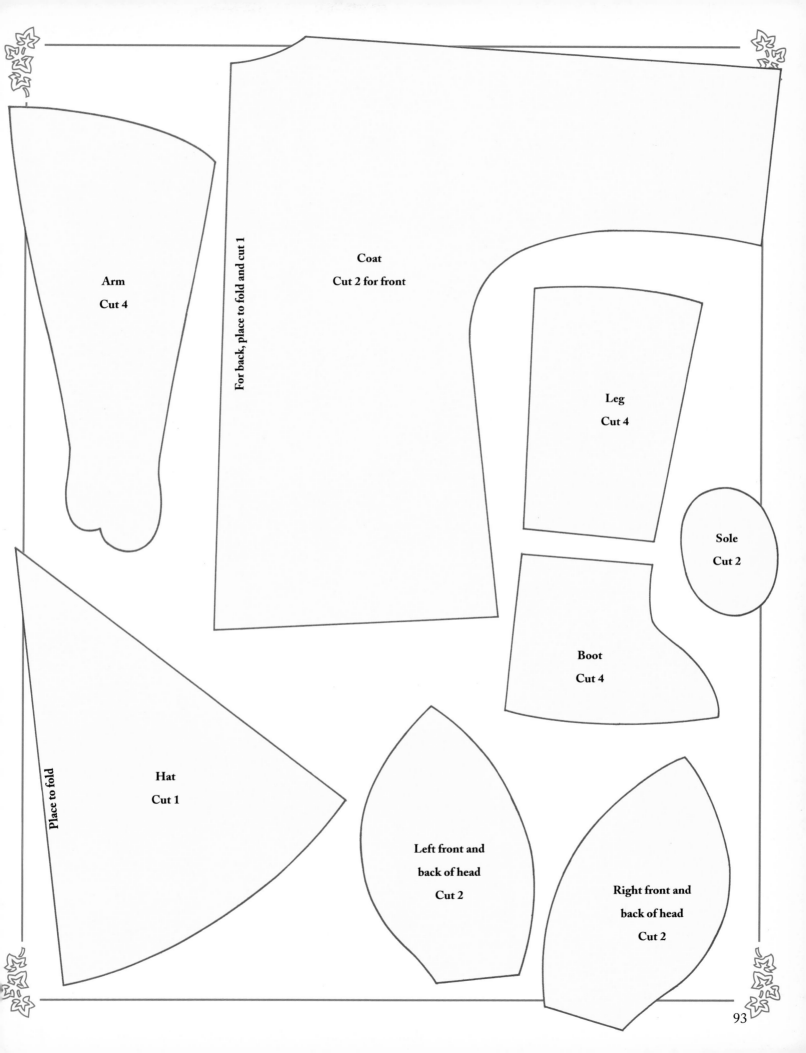

Arm
Cut 4

For back, place to fold and cut 1

Coat
Cut 2 for front

Leg
Cut 4

Sole
Cut 2

Boot
Cut 4

Place to fold

Hat
Cut 1

Left front and
back of head
Cut 2

Right front and
back of head
Cut 2

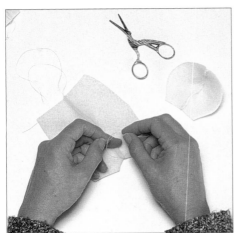

1 Stitch the right and left front body pieces together down centre seam. Repeat with back body pieces. Stitch the front head pieces together down centre seam. Repeat with back head pieces.

2 Join the front head to the front body at the neck. Cut off any loose threads. Repeat with the back head and body pieces.

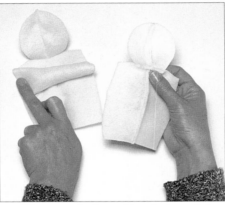

3 Place two arm pieces on top of each other and stitch together, leaving the shoulder open. Repeat with the other two arm pieces. Turn right side out and stuff with kapok.

4 Place one body and head piece right side up. Place one arm on top and then place the second body and head piece on top of this, right side down.

5 Stitch along the side seam of the doll to join all three pieces together. Fasten off any loose threads.

6 Repeat with the other arm, then turn the doll inside out. Tack from the edge of one shoulder around the head to the other shoulder, making sure that you do not tack through the doll's arms.

ABOVE: *Felt is the perfect fabric for projects such as this: it is inexpensive to buy, it comes in a wide range of colours and – possibly most important of all for the amateur or inexperienced stitcher – it does not fray.*

7 Machine stitch around the head and shoulders. Turn the doll right side out and stuff with kapok.

8 Sew the leg and boot pieces together down the long sides, leaving the top and bottom open. Oversew the soles onto the boots. Repeat the process for the other leg.

ABOVE: *Using fabric glue and a fine paintbrush, glue on the tiny felt pieces for the eyes and mouth. If you plan to give this Father Christmas doll to young children, make sure the glue is non-toxic.*

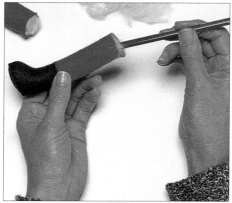

9 Stuff the legs with kapok, using the point of a pencil to push down the kapok into the boot if necessary.

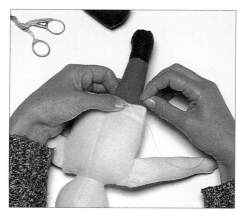

10 Tack around the bottom edge and hand stitch the legs in position, making sure they both face the same way. Oversew the bottom edge of the doll to close any remaining gaps.

11 Dip a fine brush in fabric glue and glue on the felt pieces for the eyes and mouth. Glue on cotton wool for the hair, eyebrows and moustache.

12 Stitch the front coat pieces to the back piece along the shoulder and side seams. Stitch along the back seam of the hat, turn right side out and sew on the bobble.

13 Cut a narrow strip of white felt and glue it to the cuffs and the bottom and front edges of the coat. Trim the bottom edge of the hat with white felt in the same way.

14 Dress the doll in the coat. Glue on the hat. Cut a brown felt strip for the belt. Cut two slits in a white felt square for the buckle and feed the belt through it.

Christmas Stocking

Hang up this colourful Christmas stocking for Father Christmas to fill with goodies. You can make the stocking any size you like: just enlarge or reduce the templates on a photocopier and remember to adjust the amount of other materials accordingly.

MATERIALS

For the stocking:

Two 12-in (30-cm) squares of green felt

•

6-in (15-cm) length of green ribbon,
$1/2$ in (1 cm) wide, for loop

•

1 yd (1 m) red ribbon, $1/4$ in (6 mm) wide, for edging

For the cuff and decoration:

12-in (30-cm) square of white felt

•

12-in (30-cm) square of green felt

•

2 gold star-shaped sequins

•

4 gold or silver bells

•

Gold or silver sequins or beads

•

4 pompoms in contrasting colours

•

18-in (45-cm) length of red ribbon,
$1/4$ in (6 mm) wide

•

12-in (30-cm) length of green ribbon,
$1/4$ in (6 mm) wide

LEFT: *Brightly coloured pompoms and a red ribbon edging provide the finishing touches to this stocking. For the cuff decorations, experiment with other decorative details such as the cherub shown on pages 49–49 or one of the cross-stitch motifs on pages 52–53.*

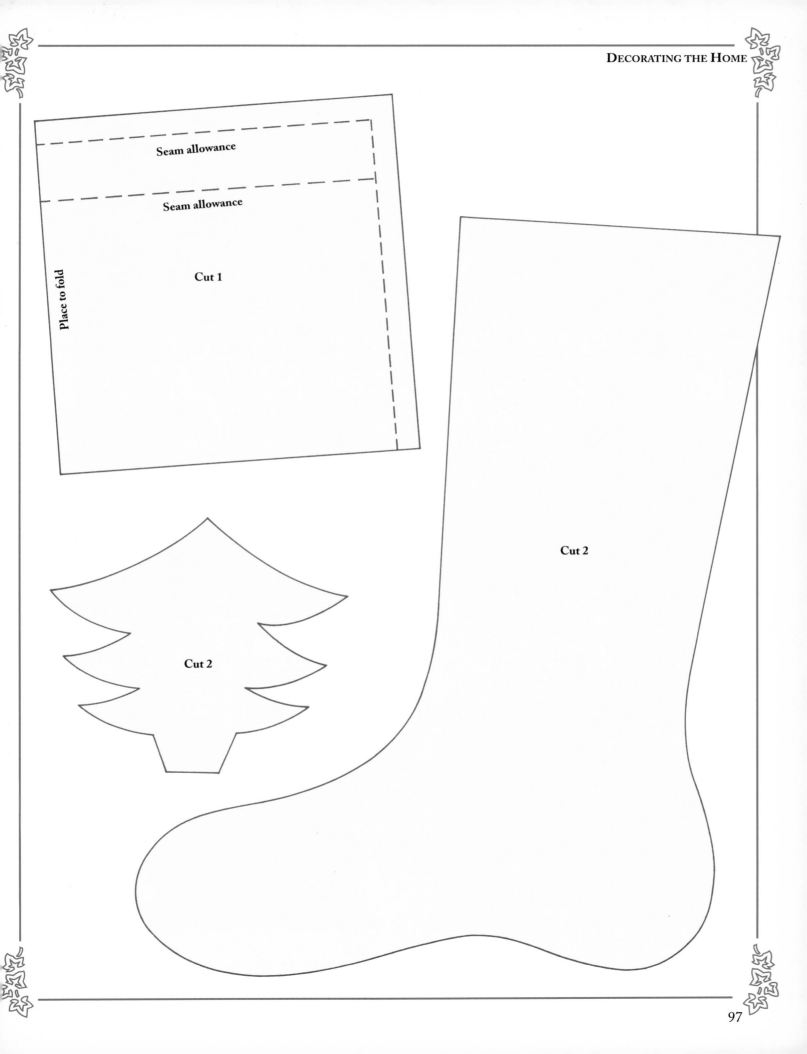

Seam allowance

Seam allowance

Place to fold

Cut 1

Cut 2

Cut 2

BELOW: *Decorate the Christmas trees on the stocking cuff with any tiny beads, bells and stars that you have in your sewing box to add colour and sparkle.*

1 Cut two stocking pieces from the template on page 97. Place them together and stitch around the edge, leaving the top open. Cut one white felt cuff piece from the template on page 97.

2 Cut two tree shapes from green felt and decorate with ribbon twists, gold stars and silver and gold bells or beads as for the Christmas trees on pages 44–45. Appliqué them to the cuff.

3 Place the top of the cuff around the top edge of the stocking, right sides together, and stitch in place. Trim the excess felt level with the back seam.

4 Turn down the cuff. Stitch a green ribbon loop to the back seam. Thread a large-eyed sharp needle with narrow red ribbon and overstitch around the edge of the stocking.

5 Sew a pompom to each end of the green and red ribbons, pulling the thread through the centre of the pompoms. Fasten off the thread to secure.

6 Fold the pompom ribbons in half and stitch them together about 1 in (2.5 cm) from their centre fold. Stitch to the back seam of the stocking.

ZIG-ZAG CUFF DECORATION

LEFT: *This zig-zag cuff, with its lattice of red and green ribbons, is an unusual variation on the basic stocking shown on the previous pages. Have fun creating your own decorations.*

Seam allowance

Place to fold

Seam allowance

Cut 1 from each colour of felt

MATERIALS

12-in (30-cm) square of patterned white felt (top cuff)

•

12-in (30-cm) square of red felt (bottom cuff)

•

Red and green ribbon, 1/8 in (3 mm) wide, to trim top cuff

•

2 large gold bells and 12 small silver and gold bells

•

12-in (30-cm) length of red ribbon, 1/4 in (6 mm) wide

•

14-in (35-cm) length of green ribbon, 1/4 in (6 mm) wide

•

22-in (55-cm) length of red ribbon, 1/4 in (6 mm) wide

1 Using the template above, cut the top cuff piece from patterned white felt. Hold firmly while cutting the zig-zags so that the felt does not slip.

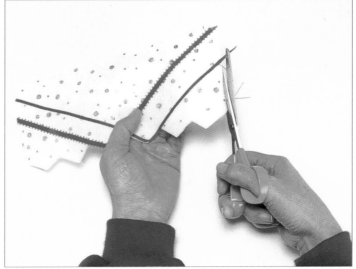

2 Stitch red and green ribbon diagonally across the cuff, using the points of the zig-zag pattern to get the angles right. Trim off the ends to neaten.

3 Continue until the zig-zag pattern is complete, trimming off any excess ribbon and threads to neaten.

4 Cut another cuff piece from the red felt. Stitch along the centre back seam. Fold the ribbon-decorated cuff in half, right sides together, and stitch along the centre back seam.

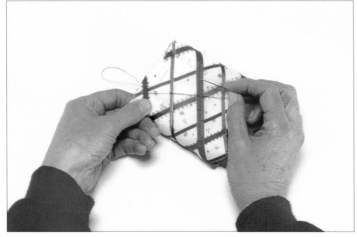

5 Turn both cuffs right side out. Place the red cuff inside the white one. Pull it down slightly and arrange the zig-zags evenly. Align the centre back seams and tack together.

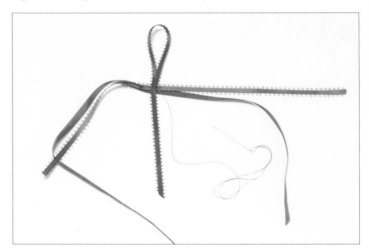

6 Fold the 12-in (30-cm) length of red ribbon in half to form a loop and stitch it onto the remaining lengths of red and green ribbon at right angles, 3 in (7.5 cm) from the fold.

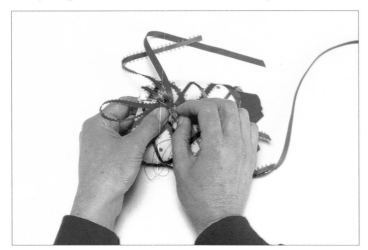

7 Stitch the ribbon decoration to the centre back seam of the cuff, stitching through the centre of the loop. Fasten off any loose threads.

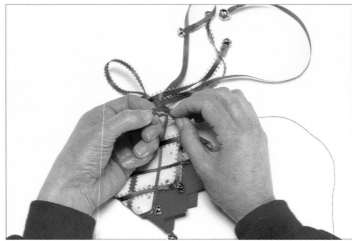

8 Stitch bells to the points of the cuffs and to the ends of the ribbons, alternating between gold and silver bells if you wish. Attach the cuff to the stocking (see step 3 on page 98).

Ivy Streamers

These ivy streamers are a novel solution to the perennial problem of how to display Christmas cards. Adapt the idea to make a decorative swag for a dado rail or banister.

MATERIALS

Long strands of ivy (*Hedera* sp.)

•

Reel wire

•

Two 12-in (30-cm) sprigs of variegated leaves with berries

•

6 pomegranate shells, sprayed gold

•

Medium-gauge florist's wire

•

Two 32-in (80-cm) lengths of wired blue-green chiffon ribbon, 1½ in (4 cm) wide

Two 18-in (45-cm) lengths of wired red ribbon, 2½ in (6 cm) wide

•

Two pieces of veiling or white net, 4 in (10 cm) wide, approximately the same length as the height of the door

•

Two pieces of wired blue-green chiffon ribbon, 1½ in (4 cm) wide, approximately the same length as the height of the door

BELOW: *Bright red ribbon is used to make a flamboyant bow for the corners of the decoration. It picks up the colour of the berries in the central spray of variegated leaves.*

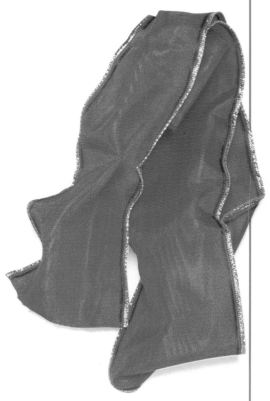

1 Drape ivy around the door, securing at the top and corners by gently tapping tacks into the door frame. Wire in extra lengths of ivy by wrapping reel wire around the stems.

2 Continue until you have covered the entire length of the door and the ivy streamers are of the desired thickness. Gently tweak the leaves so that as many as possible face forwards.

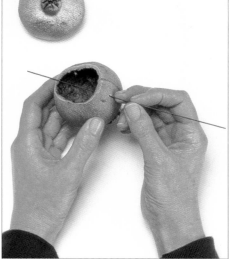

3 Place two sprigs of variegated leaves together, with the cut ends overlapping. Join together by winding reel wire around the cut ends. Position at the centre top of the door.

4 Make a small hole in the side of each dried pomegranate. Push through a length of medium-gauge florist's wire and bend one end back flat against the fruit. Wire six pomegranates in this way.

5 Hold three wired pomegranates firmly together. Twist a length of medium-gauge florist's wire around the stems and between each fruit to make a secure bunch.

6 Take a 32-in (80-cm) length of wired blue-green ribbon and twist it around the pomegranates, bringing both ends up above the fruit. Tie in a four-looped bow (see p. 126).

7 Take an 18-in (45-cm) length of wired red ribbon and tie in a two-looped bow (see p. 126). Attach behind the pomegranate bunch. Make another pomegranate bunch in the same way.

8 Take one length of veiling and one length of blue-green ribbon and tie together. Hang down one side of the door over the ivy. Repeat on the other side of the door.

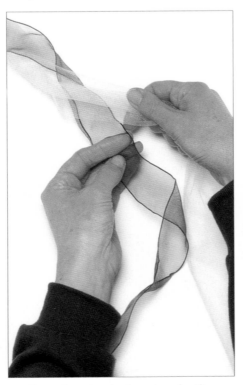

9 Loosely twist the lengths of veiling and ribbon over each other and knot together at the base. Fix one pomegranate bunch to each corner of the door frame.

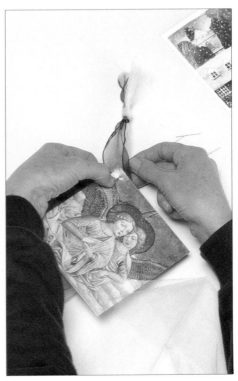

10 Using dress-making pins, pin Christmas cards down the length of the ribbon twists. If you have very young children, it is safer to glue the cards in place.

Fireplace Garland

This attractive garland is made almost entirely from dried and artificial leaves and flowers, so it will hold its shape and colour throughout the festive season. You may need to make a few minor adjustments once the garland has been hung above the fireplace.

ABOVE: *Dried grape vine, available from florist's shops, forms the base of this garland. The quantities below make a garland approximately 9 feet (3 metres) long; measure the area above your fireplace to determine how much grape vine you need.*

MATERIALS

9-foot (3-metre) length of dried grape vine

•

Medium-gauge florist's wire

•

Two 36-in (90-cm) lengths of wired gold ribbon, 2¼ in (6 cm) wide

•

9 poinsettia heads (artificial)

•

12 white hellebore flowers (artificial)

•

4 white roses (artificial)

•

10–15 sprigs of red and green leaves (artificial)

•

14–16 dried hydrangea heads

•

8 larch or other large cones, sprayed gold

•

8 yellow and 2 brown paper roses

•

1 bunch Chinese lanterns

•

6 sprigs red berries (artificial)

•

4 bunches fresh mistletoe (*Viscum album*)

•

6 bunches fresh variegated ivy (*Hedera* sp.)

1 Wet the dried grape vine and stretch it out to the required shape on a piece of hard board, using a nail in each corner to secure it. Leave to dry for a day or two.

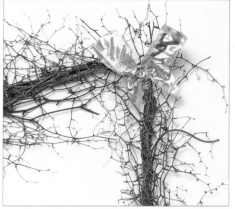

2 Push a 14-in (35-cm) length of medium-gauge florist's wire through the top corner, bend it into a circle and twist the wire ends together to form a loop. Repeat at the other corner.

3 Tie a length of wired gold ribbon around the top corner of the garland, making sure that you do not cover or obstruct the wire loop. Repeat in the other corner.

4 Tie the ribbon into a neat bow at each corner. Trim the ends to neaten if necessary and arrange attractively.

5 Place a large poinsettia head in the middle of the garland and, using a glue gun, fix it in position. Press lightly onto the garland with your fingertips until it is securely fixed.

6 Place a small poinsettia head on either side of the large one and glue into position.

7 Glue a large poinsettia head under each corner bow. Glue smaller poinsettia heads halfway down and at the bottom of each side of the garland.

8 Place one white hellebore flower on either side of the large poinsettia head at the top of the garland and glue in place.

9 Place a white rose under each white hellebore and glue into position.

10 On each side, glue one white hellebore on either side of the corner poinsettia and one white hellebore under the middle poinsettia. Glue one white rose beneath the corner poinsettias.

ABOVE: *White roses and hellebores have been used in this garland to contrast with the rich colours of the other ingredients. If you can't get hold of exactly the same flowers, substitute any other light-coloured flower of a similar size.*

11 On each side of the garland, glue one white hellebore halfway between the central motif and the corner.

12 Glue sprigs of artificial red leaves between the central motif and each corner.

13 Glue two dried hydrangea heads above the central motif.

14 Glue the rest of the hydrangea heads around the garland, distributing them evenly but without trying to be rigidly symmetrical. You will probably need about 14–16 hydrangea heads in total.

15 Glue one cone on either side of the central motif and three down each side. (As the cones are quite heavy, glue both the stalks and the cones themselves.)

16 Glue a yellow paper rose on either side of the central motif. Glue a bunch of 3 roses (2 yellow, 1 brown) halfway down each side, and a single yellow rose at the bottom.

17 Glue 4–5 small sprigs of Chinese lanterns to each side, spacing them fairly evenly. Add sprigs of artificial berries to the sides and centre, wherever you feel extra colour is needed.

18 Insert a few artificial green leaves where necessary for colour contrast. Take four bunches of berried mistletoe and glue them in a fan shape under the central motif.

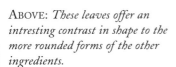

ABOVE: *These leaves offer an interesting contrast in shape to the more rounded forms of the other ingredients.*

19 Take six small bunches of variegated ivy. Glue one bunch on either side of the mistletoe, one in each corner, and one halfway down each side.

Decorated Log Basket

Designed to match the Fireplace Garland on pages 104–107, the warm reds and oranges of the poinsettia leaves and Chinese lanterns echo the fire's flames and embers. Make sure the decoration is not so large that it overshadows the basket.

ABOVE: *An artificial ponsettia head forms the focal point of this decoration. If you can't find one, substitute any large-headed, brightly coloured flower or leaf bract.*

MATERIALS

Medium-gauge florist's wire

•

1 poinsettia head (fabric)

•

2 white hellebore flowers (fabric)

•

2 large cones, sprayed gold

•

5 paper roses (3 yellow, 2 brown)

•

2 small sprigs Chinese lanterns, 2–3 lanterns per sprig

•

6–10 green poinsettia leaves (fabric)

1 Wire each item with a short length of medium-gauge florist's wire, wrapping it around the base or stem of each one. Leave about 4 in (10 cm) of wire protruding.

2 Fix the poinsettia head to the centre front of the basket by pushing the wires through, twisting them together and then bending them back to lie flat against the basket.

3 Attach one white hellebore flower on each side of the poinsettia head and secure in the same way.

4 Attach the two gold cones securely under the hellebore flowers.

5 Wire two yellow and one brown paper rose into a bunch and attach them between the cones. Make sure the bunch of roses is positioned centrally under the poinsettia head.

6 Wire together the remaining two paper roses and attach them to the basket just above the poinsettia head.

7 Attach the two sprigs of Chinese lanterns to the basket, one on the outer side of each white hellebore flower.

8 Attach the green fabric leaves, distributing them evenly around the base of the floral decoration.

RIGHT: *The success of this project depends on having one large element and just enough decorative detail to contrast with the natural wicker of the basket and the coals and logs piled up inside it.*

Rose-Scented Wreath

This unusual heart-shaped wreath is lightly scented with the warm, subtle fragrance of rose oil. Made entirely from artificial leaves and flowers and crowned by a golden bird and a subtle pink ribbon, it would make an elegant adornment to any internal door.

1 Draw a large heart to use as a template. Following your template, bend the fencing wire in the middle to form the point at the base of the heart.

2 Still following your template, bend the wire into the heart shape, working from the bottom to the top of the heart.

MATERIALS

48 in (120 cm) fencing wire

•

Cotton thread

•

Gutta percha

•

Length of artificial ivy at least 48 in (120 cm) long

Length of artificial pine cones at least 48 in (120 cm) long

3 sprigs artificial berries

•

3 artificial roses

•

Perfumed rose oil

•

Medium-gauge florist's wire

•

Artificial bird, sprayed gold

•

2 yds (2 m) wired pink chiffon ribbon, 1¹/₂ in (4 cm) wide

BELOW: *Artificial and silk roses can look very natural. Here, they are lightly scented with rose oil, which can be bought from aromatherapy suppliers.*

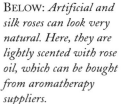

RIGHT: *The delicate pink roses complement the green ivy base perfectly. Small rosebuds are ideal for this project: the wreath is very fine and a heavy-headed flower would unbalance the overall effect.*

3 Overlap the wires at the top of the heart and bind them firmly together with cotton thread.

4 Wrap gutta percha around the heart-shaped frame, making sure you cover the wire completely. Gutta percha is self-adhesive, so you do not need to stick it to the frame.

5 Wind artificial ivy around the frame. Adjust the position of the leaves as you work so that they fan out attractively and hide the gutta percha as much as possible.

6 Wind the length of pine cones around the frame. (If you cannot find a ready-made length, wire six individual pairs of gold-sprayed cones to the wreath.)

7 Space the artificial berry sprigs evenly around the wreath and attach them by twisting their stems around the wreath base. Hide the ends of the stems under the ivy leaves.

8 Using a dropper or a fine-tipped brush, coat the inner petals of each rose with perfumed rose oil.

RIGHT: *Lengths of artificial ivy can be bought from good department stores and garden centres. They are easy to manipulate and bend to the shape you want and, unlike fresh ivy, will not dry out.*

9 Space the roses evenly around the wreath, roughly halfway between the sprigs of berries, and attach them to the wreath by twisting their stems around the frame.

10 Use medium-gauge florist's wire to attach the bird to the top of the wreath, making sure it is firmly bound in place. Cover the wire with a piece of gutta percha.

11 Loop the ribbon around the top of the wreath, making sure it is properly centred. Knot the ribbon ends just above the frame, behind the bird.

12 To make a loop for hanging the wreath, measure up 9 in (23 cm) from the knot and tie another knot. Then tie the two loose ends of the ribbon in a bow.

13 Tie the two loose ends of the bow into another bow which lies diagonally across the first one. Trim the ends of the ribbon to neaten.

Christmas Welcome Wreath

This traditional–style Christmas wreath, designed to welcome visitors to your home over the festive period, is made from winter's finest foliage: holly, mistletoe and ivy.

ABOVE AND RIGHT: *Gold bows and bells lend a festive contrast to the opulent evergreens. You may need to make minor adjustments to the overall shape of the wreath once it is in position on the door.*

MATERIALS

Wreath base, 20 in (50 cm) in diameter

•

14-in (35-cm) length of heavy-gauge florist's wire,

•

Ivy (*Hedera* sp.)

•

Medium-gauge florist's wire

Variegated holly (*Ilex* sp.)

•

6 sprigs of small artificial berries

•

Mistletoe (*Viscum album*)

•

9 pine cones (*Pinus* sp.), lightly sprayed white

Dark green holly (*Ilex* sp.)

•

3–5 sprigs of large artificial berries

•

30-in (75-cm) length of gold ribbon, 1/2 in (12 mm) wide

•

9 small gold bells

1 Push a 14-in (35-cm) length of heavy-gauge florist's wire through the wreath base and bend both ends upwards.

2 Bend the wires round several times into a circle to form a loop for hanging and twist the excess wire around the base of the loop to fasten it securely.

3 Take 4–5 sprigs of ivy, 9 in (22.5 cm) in length, and wire into a bunch with medium-gauge florist's wire. Leave 2–3 in (5–7.5 cm) of wire protruding. Make 12 bunches.

4 Fasten the ivy bunches to the wreath base by twisting the protruding length of wire around twigs in the base. All the bunches should face the same way.

5 Continue until the base is completely covered with ivy, overlapping the bunches so that the wires are hidden and there are no large gaps.

6 Take 2–3 sprigs of variegated holly, 6 in (15 cm) in length, and a small sprig of artificial berries. Twist wire around the stems, leaving 2–3 in (5–7.5 cm) protruding. Make 6 bunches.

7 Space the variegated holly bunches evenly around the base and fasten them to the base in the same way as the ivy bunches (see step 4).

8 Wire 5–6 sprigs of mistletoe, 9 in (22.5 cm) in length, leaving 2–3-in (5–7.5-cm) of wire protruding. Position four mistletoe bunches evenly around the wreath.

9 Wrap medium-gauge florist's wire around the base of each pine cone and twist to secure. Make three clusters of three cones each by twisting their wires together.

ABOVE AND BELOW: *The seasonal white berries of the kissing plant, mistletoe (top), and the golden colour of the variegated ivy (bottom) help to give light and contrast to this traditional Christmas wreath.*

10 Wire the pine cone clusters onto the wreath. Take a 5-in (12.5-cm) sprig of dark green holly and a small sprig of artificial berries and wire together. Make 3–5 bunches.

11 Attach the holly and berry bunches to the wreath wherever a splash of extra colour is needed.

12 Cut the gold ribbon into three equal lengths. Join three bells together by threading ribbon through their loops and tying in a neat bow. Make three bell clusters in total.

13 Push medium-gauge florist's wire through the loops of the bells and twist to secure. Attach the bells to the wreath, spacing them evenly.

14 Trim off any untidy-looking twigs or leaves, and fill any gaps in the wreath with extra sprigs of foliage.

Citrus Christmas Tree

*This colourful alternative to the traditional Christmas tree is
ideal for small apartments where it can sit on a shelf or window sill.
Richly adorned with artificial fruit and berries, a gold star and a
ribbon bow provide the luxuriant finishing touches.*

MATERIALS

Terracotta pot 6 in (15 cm) in diameter,
sprayed gold

•

1 small block of florist's clay

•

1 dry oasis cone, 12 in (30 cm) high x 4 in
(10 cm) in diameter at base

•

4–5 birch twigs approx.
6–8 in (15–20 cm) in length

•

1 block of dry oasis

•

Lichen moss

•

25–30 artificial poinsettia leaves, lightly
sprayed with a little gold paint

•

Glue gun

•

All-purpose glue

•

A selection of artificial miniature fruit and
berries – peaches, plums, apples, red berries,
rose hips

•

Curls of dried citrus peel (see page 127)

•

Gold ribbon curls (see page 127)

•

Gold star, 3 in (7.5 cm) high

•

30-in (75-cm) length of wired gold chiffon
ribbon, 3 in (7.5 cm) wide

LEFT: *Choose fruits that give
a good mix of seasonal colours and are
not too large. You can buy artificial
fruit and leaves in department
stores and garden centres, though you
will probably need to trim them
down to the right size.*

1 Take a small block of florist's clay and knead it in your hands until it is soft and pliable enough to mould to the shape you want.

2 Press the clay firmly and evenly into the bottom of the pot. The block of clay should come at least one third of the way up the pot as it forms the foundations of the arrangement. It will set hard within a couple of days.

3 Using a scalpel, cut a small hole about 1½ in (4 cm) deep in the base of the oasis cone. This makes it easier to insert the birch twig 'tree trunk' at the next stage.

BELOW: *The peel curls can be made from any citrus fruit – lime, lemon, orange or grapefruit. Citrus peel curls into naturally interesting shapes as it dries, offering a visual contrast to the rounded shapes of the fruits. It also has a wonderfully seasonal fragrance.*

4 Push one thick birch twig into the hole in the oasis, making sure the cone is firmly wedged onto the twig. Make sure the birch twig is centrally positioned.

5 Push thinner twigs into the oasis cone around the main twig to create a really sturdy trunk'. Wedge the trunk firmly into the florist's clay at the bottom of the pot.

6 Cut small pieces from an oasis block and use them to fill in around the trunk, pushing them firmly down into the pot. Check from time to time to make sure that the trunk and the oasis cone remain vertical as you work.

7 Spread lichen moss around the base of the trunk, making sure the oasis is completely covered.

BELOW: The rose hips and berries, with their vibrant reds, give a wonderful lift to the tree. Don't use too many berries: red is a very dominant colour and, if overused, it could easily overwhelm the tree and disrupt the balance of colours.

8 Starting from the bottom of the oasis cone and working upwards, glue artificial poinsettia leaves over the cone, overlapping the leaves slightly but taking care not to pack them too tightly together.

9 Continue until you have completely covered the oasis cone. The gold spray on the leaves gives a luxuriant feel to the arrangement.

10 Start adding the plums, spacing them randomly around the tree and using a glue gun to fix them in place. Remember to keep the heavier fruit around the base to prevent the tree from looking top heavy.

11 Add bunches of peaches. For the heavier fruit, bend a short length of medium-gauge florist's wire in half to form a pin and push it over the stem of the fruit into the oasis cone

12 Attach clusters of apples randomly around the tree, taking care to maintain a good conical shape.

13 Insert red berries and sprigs of rose hips evenly over the tree. Check periodically to make sure that the tree remains truly vertical.

14 Add the citrus peel and gold ribbon curls, allowing the ribbon to drop naturally around the other fruit and foliage.

15 Glue the star securely to the top of the tree, making sure that one tip points upwards.

16 Put a dab of glue on the back of the pot and attach the gold ribbon just under the rim, tying it in a neat two-looped bow (see page 126). Make sure the size of the ribbon is in proportion to the pot and the tree.

Fan-Shaped Tree

This alternative Christmas tree was inspired by Japanese flower arrangements. The colour scheme is limited and the structure minimalist, but it is the vibrant orangey-gold of the Chinese lanterns that catches the eye.

1 Insert the florist's clay into the bottom of the pot and press down firmly. (Unlike oasis, florist's clay does not crumble and will set hard within a couple of days.)

2 Place the pot in the middle of the hessian square and round off the shape by cutting away the corners. Using a glue gun, dab glue around the inside top edge of the pot.

3 Fold the hessian up over the rim of the pot, gathering it evenly as you go, and press it firmly against the glued inside edge until it has stuck fast.

MATERIALS

Terracotta pot, 4 in (10 cm) in diameter
•
Florist's clay
•
14 x 14 in (35 x 35 cm) piece of hessian
•
Glue gun
•
All-purpose glue
•
1 bunch of natural birch twigs
•
1 bunch of birch twigs, sprayed silvery-white
•
1 bunch of Chinese lanterns
•
1 bunch of natural honesty
•
1 bunch of honesty, sprayed gold
•
18-in (45-cm) length of green paper ribbon

RIGHT: *The orange and gold colours of this arrangement stand out best against a plain background.*

4 Position one natural birch twig in the middle of the pot, pressing it down firmly into the clay. Place four or five other birch twigs loosely around it, establishing the basic fan shape of the arrangement.

5 Insert 8–10 silvery-white birch twigs between the natural birch twigs. The exact position is not important, but try to distribute them evenly so that the arrangement looks balanced. All the twigs should be roughly the same length.

6 Insert 3–4 sprigs of Chinese lanterns around the front of the arrangement. Do not use too many: the colour is very strong and the arrangement could easily look garish.

ABOVE: *Chinese lanterns have a wonderfully rich, orangey-gold colour. Like the honesty used in this arrangement, they are semi-transparent and would look magnificent displayed on a window ledge with the light filtering through them.*

7 Insert 3-4 stems of natural honesty, distributing them evenly throughout the arrangement. The papery leaves are similar in texture to the Chinese lanterns and form an effective contrast to the hard birch twigs.

8 Insert 6-8 stems of gold honesty, distributing them evenly throughout the arrangement. The colour subtly reinforces the warm hues of the Chinese lanterns without overpowering them.

9 Trim the twigs and stems if necessary, so that the arrangement looks evenly balanced, and fill any obvious gaps.

10 Tie the green paper ribbon around the centre of the pot, using a double knot. The ribbon and hessian are both rough in texture and this complements the natural materials used in the arrangement very well.

RIGHT: *The bulk of this arrangement is provided by birch twigs, some left plain, some sprayed silvery-white. Make sure that all the twigs you use are roughly the same length – about 20 in (50 cm) for this size of pot. The stems of honesty, too, should be about this length.*

11 Fill the pot with tiny twists of paper ribbon so that the florist's clay and the roughly cut hessian around the inner rim are hidden from view.

Finishing Techniques

TYING A TWO-LOOPED BOW

1 Take a length of decorative ribbon and tie it securely around the package. Hold one end of ribbon in each hand.

2 Make a loop with one end of the ribbon and hold it firmly in one hand, close to the package.

3 Wind the loose end of ribbon around the first loop.

4 Feed the loose ribbon through the first loop and pull tightly to form a second loop. Trim ends to neaten.

TYING A FOUR-LOOPED BOW

1 Take a long length of decorative ribbon and tie it around the package, pulling it taut. Hold one end of ribbon in each hand.

2 As in making a two-looped bow, make a small loop with one end of the ribbon and hold it firmly.

3 Make a two-looped bow as previously and adjust the loops to the same size, leaving long ends of ribbon.

4 Place the free ends of ribbon at right angles to the first two loops.

5 Make a third loop with one of the free ends of ribbon. Make a second bow with the remaining ribbon.

6 Adjust the loops to the same size, making sure that they do not overlap each other, and trim off any excess ribbon if necessary to neaten.

MAKING RIBBON CURLS

   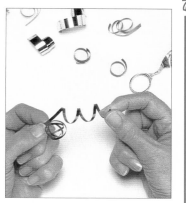

1 Take a piece of parcel ribbon and cut along its length, stopping ¹/₂ in (1 cm) short of the top.

2 Hold the uncut end of ribbon in one hand and run a scissors blade along one ribbon strand.

3 Repeat with the second ribbon strand. The more firmly you press the blade onto the ribbon, the tighter the curl will be.

4 Tweak the ribbon curl to achieve the desired effect. If the curl is too tight, you can loosen it by gently pulling.

DRYING APPLE SLICES

  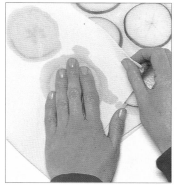 

1 Cut the unpeeled apples into slices ¹/₄ in (6 mm) thick.

2 Immerse the slices in heavily salted water for ten minutes to prevent them from discolouring.

3 Remove the apple slices from the salted water and dry on kitchen paper, dabbing them gently to absorb any excess moisture.

4 Pierce each slice with a threaded needle. Tie a knot between each slice to separate them. Hang to dry in a warm place for 3–4 days.

DRYING CITRUS PEEL

1 Using a sharp knife, cut a spiral of peel from the fruit. Try not to break the spiral if you can help it.

2 Leave in a warm, dry place for two to three days. The peel will dry to a hard, brittle finish, curling slightly as it dries.

Acknowledgements

*I would like to thank the following people for their
much-appreciated help with this book:*

The Directors of Collins & Brown; Sarah Hoggett,
whose hard work and enthusiasm have been an
inspiration; photographer Matthew Ward, assisted by
Ashley Straw and Kirstie Ashton-Bell; Deirdre Mitchell
for her help in typing the text; Suzanne Metcalfe-
Megginson for design assistance in the early stages of
the book's production; and Adrian Waddington of
Watermark and Claire Graham for their DTP skills.

Special thanks go to Shirley Coleby for her creative skill
and support in helping to make the projects, and to
Helen Parsons and Beryl Miller. Illustrator David Ashby
provided all the artwork for the stencil designs
and templates.

Finally, my thanks to James and Anne Capon for
allowing us to photograph their home, and to Tim Page,
Barry Sartin, and Peter Jones department store of Sloane
Square, London SW1 for their very generous loan
of props.